THE UNIVERSAL JESUS

Here is the genuine beginning in modern times of what has come to be the deepest note of present-day Christianity, **the appreciation of personality as the highest thing in earth or heaven,** *and the initiation of a movement to find the vital sources and resources for the inner kindling of the spirit, and for raising the whole personal life to higher functions and to higher powers.*

Rufus M. Jones
Spiritual Reformers in the 16th and 17th centuries

The Universal Jesus

by

Meg Chignell

Sessions Book Trust
York, England

ISBN 1 85072 067 3

Printed on recycled paper in 10/11 point Plantin typeface
by William Sessions Limited
The Ebor Press, York, England

Foreword

by

Roger C. Wilson

Emeritus Professor of Education, University of Bristol

———

LIKE MANY OF MY CONTEMPORARIES, we are ready to call ourselves Christians for want of any better designation for the puzzlingly mixed religious company we keep. (For the forgotten origin of the designation, see page 111 of this book.) For myself, I have an ineffable, hot-blooded, affectionate devotion to Jesus, associated with a sense of guilty failure and the hope of forgiveness. For he was a man who did and said things, usually unconventional, unforgettably interesting – for and against – whose very unconventionality led to crucifixion. Mark leaves his story with a bleak account of the empty tomb where the guardian told the women to go to tell Peter. But they ran away and 'said nothing to anyone for they were afraid.' Mark makes no convincing reference to the resurrection experience. He offers no explanations.

It is a strong story as Mark tells it. Every element, if understood in the cultural setting of the time, is as mightily relevant to the human condition in our culture today as it was to those among whom Jesus ministered in love through deed and word.

But in a very short time after Mark had written, other New Testament writers had picked up his story, added their own accounts of before and after, together with their explanations. From these explanations have emerged the Christ of the creeds, with which, again like many of my fellow Christians, I am not at home; nor with the Christ of many well-known hymns. I am even more alienated from the Christ called in support of historical human conflict, nationalist, tribal, sexist, political, economic, . . . often buttressed by a text or two; the Christ who is, often, a symbol of complacent, self-righteous salvation. But there is the other Christ – of the faith sustaining Francis of Assisi, Eric Liddell (of Chariots of Fire), Dietrich Bonhoeffer, hanged by the Nazis in 1945, Mother Theresa, Trevor Huddleston, Desmond Tutu and countless others who have known suffering and enjoyed liberation through this elusive Christ of faith.

Need we, like the women and Mark, be afraid of what there is to know, however deep the mystery? In this illuminating book, Meg Chignell comes readably to our aid. 'The New Testament documents', she writes, 'are a record of a living encounter with the Jesus of Nazareth who becomes Jesus the Christ.' The very differences of the gospel styles sharpen the element of encounter. In an extended study of Mark, Meg discerns a totally human Jesus whose spiritual stature and unconventionality fascinate Mark and move him deeply, but leave him puzzled by what it is all about. On a humble and minute scale we can feel at home with Mark's Jesus. He is a splendid neighbour and controversialist in Galilee, a remarkably courageous person in the harsh climate of Jerusalem. But the Jesus of Mark's gospel would not have changed the world. Perhaps that is why some of us are comfortable with him.

What Meg does is to build a bridge, out of critical thought and living experience, between the Jesus of Nazareth and the Christ of faith. She crosses to and fro, refreshing herself on either bank as she needs the human Jesus or the Christ, or indeed exchanges reflections with them both in the middle.

Those who want to begin by seeing the bridge will do well to glance at the last five pages of Chapter XV, from the bottom of page 109 to the end. They may then find they want to join those who have already enjoyed the sense of creation with which she handles the girders, the wires, the nuts and bolts provided by the craftsmen, the women of many occupations, the artists, historians, poets and fishermen who pour out their discoveries and perplexities into the untidy treasure heap of the New Testament. Some things she discards: she regrets the 'deification of Jesus which robs him of his pre-eminent right to speak with authority' to every aspect of the human condition, whose perplexities, enjoyments, disasters, triumphs, sexual experience and frustrations of all sorts, greed, generosity, love, enmity, inquisitiveness, complacency, knowledge, ignorance . . . are the common ground of all religions, whether world or local in scale.

For Meg 'Jesus was primarily an innovator' who set the minds and spirits of others working, so that within two generations of his death, there was a whole network of new or revitalised divine/human relationships, knit together by the endless thread of God's unfolding love, and already producing courageous new Christians as they founded the infant Church, 'out-living, out-dying and out-thinking' the agnostic and pagan worlds of their time.

I am not sure that she will agree with my amateur interpretation of what she has to share with all of us

vii

seekers, whether deep in or on the fringes of the Christian tradition. But to be able to call attention to the liberating quality of this book is a most satisfying privilege.

Yealand Conyers,   Roger Wilson
Lancashire. March, 1990.

Acknowledgement: My deepest gratitude as always to Barbara Windle for her constant encouragement and meticulous reading of the manuscript and to Kathleen Healey for her loving support.

All biblical quotations are from *The Revised English Bible, 1989* (unless otherwise stated), by permission of the Oxford University Press and Cambridge University Press.

Contents

Part One

Jesus according to Mark's gospel

Our Human Dilemma

AT THE END OF THE 20TH CENTURY we are facing all kinds of possibilities. On the one hand there are the marvellous technological and scientific achievements which have dramatically changed our lives and our understanding of the universe in which we live. On the other there is the environmental crisis, the enormous stockpile of nuclear weapons, world poverty, hunger, political turmoil and in some countries, oppression. It is probable also that the human population will reach eight billion by the year 2000, an explosive number in terms of adequate survival. And the majority of these problems are the direct result of humanity's ignorance, greed, fear and ruthless exploitation of the earth's natural resources.

We are a fascinating species. We have the capacity of self-awareness. We reflect upon our past and dream or plan for the future. We attempt to look at ourselves in perspective, analysing and assessing our prospects. Our development has been dependent upon our ability to adapt to all kinds of different circumstances and conditions – even to the weightlessness of spatial travel! We have the gift of moral choice, are restless, inventive, arbitrary, courageous, enduring and caring. Some of the greatest amongst us have had visions of a collective Utopia for all. And yet it would seem that we now face unprecedented possibilities of disaster, even extinction, by destroying our own habitat and that of other creatures who share it with us. Some hope lies in the fact that the few who see the issues clearly may yet be able to prevail upon the majority to act in such a way as to avert catastrophe. And, through the power of mass communication and ease of travel, ordinary people, as well as world leaders are learning to think globally.

The religious of many faiths, the philosophers, social reformers, psychologists and others have addressed themselves to these problems with varying degrees of insight. There are some who see us simply as products of systems and culture, even if they do not hold to an entirely mechanistic view of the universe and all the creatures (including humans) who inhabit our planet. Many social reformers have believed that if you want to create a better world, you must change the built-in privileges of the few and share more freely with the majority. Although there is profound truth in this, it does not seem to work out in experience as the planners had hoped. For example we have the technological and scientific skill now to feed the hungry, alleviate poverty and many of the endemic current diseases in the the Third World, but we have not the corporate moral will as yet to achieve this miracle. And human history has shown that even where old regimes have been overcome, the corrupting reins of power can turn the new ones into oppressive or at least unjust states.

Those of us who live in rich and comparatively liberal countries are saturated with commercialism. Perhaps one of the greatest deceptions of our own particular Western culture is the idea presented to us, that the good life consists in having the cash to be an avid consumer and if we do not have the money now, we can always borrow it, for a time at any rate, on very easy terms. Such limited goals are a travesty of human potential yet have their obvious successes. We appear to be so easily led and mistaken as to the source of our own well-being and happiness.

Socrates is reported by Plato as having taught that every person wished for their own good and would get it if they could. For example, if a man became a thief, it was because he believed it would benefit him. Therefore education was needed to teach men self-enlightenment so that they would pursue the highest good, which for Plato at least was a moral and intellectual goal. But the question of good and evil is more complex than would appear.

Although Paul expressed his personal conflict in terms which were appropriate for his day, his experience is a universal one: 'though the will to do good is there, the ability to effect it is not. The good which I want to do, I fail to do; but what I do is the wrong which is against my will' (*Romans 7:19–20*). He analysed three elements in his own situation: the Jewish law exposed his weakness, highlighted his inability to keep it despite his rigorous self-discipline; his unspiritual nature was governed by sin and warred against his spiritual self; he found the transforming power to become a different person through his faith in Jesus the Christ. In other words the imposition of a strict code was not enough. It simply led to loveless rectitude. He had to be inspired by something infinitely greater.

'Without contraries there is no progression,' wrote William Blake. The relevance of this truth is recognisable in our experiences of the physical, emotional and intellectual life. The ebb and flow of the natural rhythms of existence in all its manifestations is an integral part of the universe in which we live. Some kind of both opposition and attraction are essential ingredients of growth. But there has to be a right balance between the two,

xiii

otherwise destruction takes place through lack of nourishment or over stimulation. Health is the striving for an equilibrium, a harmony. But we need to understand more how cause and effect work in the heart and the mind, in the moral and spiritual spheres as well as in the physical. As our bodies seek to compensate for injury or illness so our instinct in our relationships with others is to return in kind what we receive. In the fight for liberty, the oppressed may in turn become the oppressor, or the hurt, the wounder. The desire to retaliate is automatic unless subjugation or fear of repercussion has rendered us too fearful to act, and suppression is not the answer.

We can usually accept that certain suffering is inevitable, but it is more difficult to learn the wisdom of Blake's words:

> Joy and woe are woven fine,
> A clothing for the soul divine.
> Man was made for Joy and Woe;
> And when this we rightly know,
> Thro' the World we safely go. *(Auguries of Innocence)*

What may be considered to be undeserved suffering, however, is another thing altogether and stretches us beyond our resources. Its causes are manifold but often the innocent suffer in consequence of others' evil intent, greed, selfishness, or ignorance. For example at least 6,000 people are killed each year on the roads, many of them through drunken driving. Even more are horribly injured through the same cause.

It is, of course, true that we are moulded by our past. We understand something of how we are influenced by our genes and our environment. Even so I do not believe that these influences can explain everything about us. For better or for worse, we are distinctively ourselves from our unique fingerprints to our particular physical make up and psychological traits. Any way forward, therefore, must lie in our growing understanding of ourselves, our motivations and our ability to change. We have not only to recognise this but to find the power to overcome the fundamental strand of self-deception and self-destructiveness which lies at the heart of our dilemmas. We are driven back to the problem of evil in all its forms.

Evil has been defined in many ways. It has been given the status of deity hence the ideas of the opposing forces of good and evil spirits, angels and devils, God and Satan. Dualism of this nature is an intrinsic part of the religion of Zoroaster, the Persian whose thoughts influenced not only the Pharisaic party of Jesus' day, but other neighbouring faiths. [Zoroastrianism was replaced by Islam, when Arabs conquered Persia around AD 700. It now exists mainly in India where its followers are called Parsis.]

In biblical terms Satan is finally presented as a fallen angel, not in any way the equal of God *(Revelation 12:7–9)*. I believe this symbolism holds profound truth for I see evil as misdirected energy. It can be and usually is the distortion of the good in a spiritual as well as every other sense.

In the second biblical myth of the world's creation, a human being (man) is formed from the dust, 'the Lord God breathed into his nostrils the breath of life; so that he became a living creature' *(Gen. 2:7)*. In Old Testament symbolism, the breath of God stands for his spirit which energises the soul or the life principle of humanity. The latter image, therefore, is that of a potter having the power to animate his creation by his own breath or spirit. Humanity, therefore, possessing the breath of God, has a spiritual core.

In the first creation myth there is the concept that 'God created human beings in his own image, in the image of God he created them; male and female he created them' *(Gen. 1:27)*. We do not know precisely what the writer of Genesis 1 meant by saying that we were made in God's image. But from the following verses describing man's tasks, it is clear tht he has the power of reason, of moral choice and, as God's representative, he is given lordship over the animal kingdom.

The power of moral choice, as in any other decision making process, can only be exercised when viable options present themselves. In biblical terms transgression is seen as an act of disobedience against God's directive. For example, parabolically, the first sin is presented as Eve's taking of the forbidden fruit from the Tree of Knowledge of Good and Evil. She finds this irresistible because she has been told by the Tempter that through it she will gain God-like powers and wisdom.

Pragmatically, the Law or Will of the Creator continues to be spelt out through the Covenants (or sacred agreements) which he makes with Abraham, Noah and Moses. It was inevitable that these laws should eventually contain detailed ritual regulations concerning the cult. This is usual for that period of religious history. Their uniqueness lies in the moral demands made upon his people by an ethical deity. Later the prophetic mind was able to distil from this mass of legislation, something of the nature of the God they worshipped and insights into the basic needs of humanity itself –

> He has showed you, O man, what is good;
> and what does the Lord require of you
> but to do justice, and to love kindness,
> and to walk humbly with your God   *(RSV, Micah 6:8)*.

In Jesus' time there was a great debate amongst the foremost Rabbis as to whether the ritual and ethical commands of the Law had equal merit. They counted 613 regulations in all. This controversy probably lay behind a genuine question asked of Jesus by a lawyer – 'Which is the first of all the commandments?' *(Mark 12:28)*. Jesus replies with great clarity and authority – 'The first is, "hear O Israel: the Lord our God is the one Lord; and you must love the Lord your God with all your heart, with all your soul, with all your mind, and with all your strength" ' *(Deuteronomy 6:4–5)*. 'The second is this: "Love your neighbour as yourself" ' *(Leviticus 19:18)*.

He further enhancd his teaching on the primacy of love by giving a simple rule by which to live 'Always treat others as you would like them to treat you; that is the Law and the prophets' *(Matthew 7:12)*. The negative form of this advice is found in the teaching of the Chinese sage, Confucius, 500 years before Jesus, and also in the teaching of the renowned Rabbi Hillel (a contemporary of Jesus). The additional power of the positive, however, is quite striking.

Jesus' summary of the law of God has had far reaching repercussions, many of which the historic Christian church has not yet begun to work out. But the impact of the person of Jesus upon his contemporaries can be clearly traced in the New Testament documents themselves.

The author of the first letter of John, for example, has so absorbed the Jesus event that through it, he can state categorically –

'God is Love; he who dwells in love is dwelling in God, and God in him' *(4:16)*. Earlier in the letter he has written –

'God is light, and in him there is no darkness at all' *(1:5)*.

So love and light are together used as a way of describing God, the Supreme Being, the Ultimate Reality behind all there is, has been and is yet to come. But in the epistle, the greater emphasis is on Love because of the actual encounter with Jesus and his life-giving power. I cannot see that we have as yet fully understood the implications of the statement in which Love is equated with Ultimate Reality.

Jesus himself *(Mark 2:15–17)* implied that he had come to cure the sickness of sin and he certainly deeply offended the religious leaders of his day by the public forgiving of sins, as in the case of a crippled man *(Mark 2:5)* and a woman prostitute *(Luke 7:48)*. He taught about the rule or reign of God in people's hearts and minds. He personally lived out his own teaching and broke through the circle of retaliation and revenge by forgiving his enemies, even as he was being nailed to the cross. Clearly then, when love is sovereign, the power to forgive is a reality.

He had a great personal magnetism but was not corrupted by power. He saw himself essentially as God's servant who was of necessity therefore the servant of all, come to do for others what they were unable to do for themselves. He accepted his death as a further self-offering which could effectively bring to the human situation, a new dimension. His followers believed that through him, the old dispensation between God and Israel was changed because those who believed in Jesus had become part of the differently constituted Israel: literally a new age had begun for all humanity.

Paul particularly thought of Jesus as the second Adam, the spiritual progenitor of a transformed humanity. As was natural to his era, rabbinical training and faith, Paul treated the mythical Adam of the Genesis stories, as a real historical person. He interpreted the perverseness within his own nature and his inability to overcome it, as an inherited flaw going back to that first sin of disobedience in the Garden of Eden. With the coming of Jesus whom he accepted as his Lord, he gained the insight and the power to break free from the false ideas, destructive feelings, harmful words and actions which had crippled him before. So he could write 'Do not let evil conquer you, but use good to conquer evil' *(Romans 12:21 RSV)*.

It is the power of the good, the power of compassion, the ability to see others as persons in their own right, which must continually renew humanity, for our problems are deeply spiritual in nature. Although the first step in regeneration and reformation is to understand the underlying cause of failure, the second step is to find the power and the will to act on these insights. The whole person has to be engaged. We have become alienated from the life of the spirit, from the central core of our being. We must find the way back. We need **all** the skills which are at our command to see the creative pattern in the complicated web of our humanity.

I value the bible as a whole and more particularly the New Testament because I see that it is dealing with experiential truth about humanity's quest for a religious understanding of the meaning of life. It is not and never can be, a definitive and sole source of this search because it deals with experiences of one particular people. As we learn to think globally we learn also to appreciate the many manifestations of the life of the Spirit in the different cultures and religious traditions of other races. But because our own particular Western culture is based very largely on the Judaic – Christian tradition, it is important that we understand it as fully as possible. Before we can appreciate Jesus' relevance to the late 20th century, it is necessary to try and understand the interpretations put upon his teaching, life and death by the writers of the New Testament, in particular the gospels and Paul. This can enable us to translate any fundamental biblical truth for our own time.

New Testament background

The 37 New Testament documents were practically all written within the
first century AD. The precise dates are a matter of debate and interpretation
as are also the contents! But the distance of nearly 2,000 years of human
endeavour and discovery is no mean gap and demands an imaginative
response on our part to discern the experiential truth contained in these
writings. A further problem arises from the hallowed nature of the text itself
and the ritual use to which it has been put through centuries of Christian
worship. Yet even though our culture, with its scientific and analytical mode
of thought, is very different from the first century AD, human beings
experience the same emotions whatever their cultural context.

Our knowledge of the physical universe has altered radically. People of New
Testament times (and much later) believed, from the evidence of their
senses, that the earth was flat and that the sun, moon and stars moved in
their courses in the solid dome of the sky above them. The Jews saw their
God as dwelling in glory in Heaven, which lay above that which mortal eye
could see. Other peoples thought of the heavenly bodies themselves as being
either divine or the abode of the gods. We know otherwise. But we too, can
experience wonder and awe, inspired by the immensity of outer space. We
know that it is our world which moves around the particular star which is
our sun and we have seen from cameras on our spacecrafts, the planet earth,
which is our home, floating in a sea of darkness. From our current
explorations into the nature of the universe of which we are a part, we may
have changed our perceptions of deity, but this should not make us
arrogant. Looking back on a life devoted to scientific exploration, Newton
described himself as a child playing with a few brightly coloured pebbles on
a beach, while the whole ocean of knowledge lay unexplored before him.

The Jews have had a tortuous history. At the time of Jesus they were a
subject people within the extensive Roman empire. But this was no new
thing for them. As a small and insignificant nation, living in the Fertile
Crescent, stretching from the Nile to the Euphrates, they were often caught
up in the struggles for supremacy by far greater powers. Egyptian,
Assyrian, Persian, Greek and Roman armies had fought and died in
Palestine. The unique thing about the Hebrews was their religious faith,
kept alive by the few for the many, through times of conquest and despair:
for they believed it was the one true God, the Lord of History and of Time,
who had called them to be his special people and to bear witness to him to
the nations of the world. Their varied understanding of and commitment to
this calling is the theme of the Old Testament. And for the Christian this
theme was continued and in one sense completed by the coming of Jesus the
Christ.

We know that in human history, a sense of superiority is quite common amongst different races. We still have it today. For a long period of time, also, women have been subjected to male dominance; conquered peoples have been turned into slaves; war, oppression, cruelty and force have kept in place unjust hierarchical structures. We are just beginning to see changed attitudes and practices about these matters, but there is still a long way to go. We cannot be surprised, therefore, if we find in the New Testament an acceptance of a state of affairs that we have begun to reject. This acceptance does not invalidate the reality and value of the human relationships thus described. We see courage, wit, compassion, pain, fear, sorrow and death; our shared experiences whether we lived 2,000 years ago or today. There is also, of course, what we might describe as ignorant superstition about the unknown. Illness could be attributed to demon possession or the result of a punishment for sin, whether ritual or ethical. There were no clear boundaries between what might be described as miracles or natural events – natural law as we know it, such as the law of gravity, had not been defined, yet the law still operated. But matters are surely not so very different today, for despite our sophistication and adherence to the scientific method many of us are very ignorant and consequently superstitious.

If we approach the New Testament with an imaginative response to the people who wrote and read these documents, we can be enriched. We are not being called upon to accept all their convictions and opinions unless they also ring true for us.

In previous centuries, tradition has emphasised that the bible is the word of God. It carried absolute authority and sanctity. This view is still securely held by those Christians who are known as fundamentalists or literalists. And, as a result of inadequate teaching in schools and in churches, young children can be first introduced to the bible in similar terms. Consequently many teenagers and adults believe they are faced with the option of a total acceptance or a total rejection of the bible and its faith. This is a sad state of affairs when the facts are quite otherwise. A century of intense textual scholarship, combined with archaeology and related sciences, has shown us the bible as a whole library of books written at different times with differing degrees of historical accuracy and representing various stages of spiritual development. The authors themselves had their obvious human limitations. That is why we have to seek, where we can, for experiential truth.

Historical note

Herod (known later as Herod the Great), son of Antipater, an Idumean, became king of the Jews in 37 BC. The Jewish state was regarded as a division of the Roman province of Syria. On Herod's death in 4 BC, his kingdom was divided between three of his sons. Archelaus became tetrarch of Judea, Samaria and Idumea but was deposed in AD 6. The Romans then made Judaea and Samaria into a province under a procurator. Pontius Pilate as sixth procurator was appointed about AD 25. Herod Antipas became tetrarch of Galilee and Peraea 4 BC – AD 39. He divorced his first wife, a daughter of Aretas, King of Arabia, to marry Herodias, who divorced her husband to marry Antipas. The other son, Herod Philip II became tetrarch of Iturea and Trachonitis 4 BC – AD 34.

The **Sadducees** were the aristocratic priestly class in Judaism, whose activities and authority centred upon the Temple and its services. The High Priest came from among their number. He held office through Roman patronage and was given the routine political administration of the Jewish section in Palestine. The Sadducees had a strong representation on the **Sanhedrin**, the Jewish Supreme Council in charge of local administration in Judaea. Its 70 members were drawn from high priestly families and the Rabbinical schools. It met in the Temple area. The Sadducees were very conservative in their religious outlook. Their great emphasis was on the Pentateuch, the first five books of the Old Testament. They did not believe either in life after death or that angels and spirits were active in human affairs. They were bitterly opposed to the Pharisees on these matters and did not accept the Pharisees' oral tradition.

By far the most influential group were the **Pharisees** whose devotion to the Law (in Hebrew, the **Torah**) led to their scrupulous observance of all its ritual and ethical regulations. The **Scribes** or Lawyers, usually came from the Pharisaic sect. They not only wrote out the sacred texts but discussed and interpreted their finer points. From this constant study and application came the Oral Tradition of the Elders which had considerable importance and significance. This oral tradition was later codified and written down to form the **Mishnah** around AD 200.

The **Herodians** were a worldly political party, loyal to the house of Herod the Great, whose descendants governed Palestine and surrounding areas until the Jewish war in AD 66. The Herodians believed that co-operation with Rome was essential to Jewish survival.

The **Zealots** were the extreme nationalist group in Israel, who believed in active underground resistance to the Roman occupation and who, from time to time, erupted into open rebellion.

Abbreviations: RSV – Revised Standard Version, The Division of Christian Education in the United States of America, 1946-52; The British and Foreign Bible Society, 1967. NEB – New English Bible, New Testament, O.U.P., C.U.P., 1961.

Jesus according to Mark's gospel

CHAPTER ONE

Mark

Authorship

I begin with this gospel because it is now generally agreed that it was the first to be written. In previous generations it was regarded as a pale edition of Matthew (the great teaching gospel) and therefore placed second in the New Testament. However, a comparison of the text of the three gospels, Matthew, Mark and Luke, shows that about 95% of Mark's gospel is found in Matthew and about 65% of it is found in Luke, so it is most probable that Mark's writing was known to the other two. The three gospels mentioned above are called 'the synoptics' from the Greek *syn* meaning 'together' and a verb-root associated with 'seeing'. As the three gospels follow the same general pattern, they can be arranged in parallel columns and studied together.

It is from the evidence of certain second century Christian writers, that the second gospel has been attributed to Mark. Extracts from the writing of the earliest of these, Papias, bishop of Heriapolis in Asia Minor (ca. AD 130), are recorded by Eusebius in his History of the Church. [Eusebius was bishop of Caesarea in the first half of the fourth century. His work is a mine of information about the early church.]

Papias is quoted by Eusebius as recording the tradition that 'Mark, indeed, having been the interpreter of Peter (i.e. translating Peter's Aramaic into

1

Greek), wrote accurately, howbeit not in order, all that he (Peter) recalled of what was either said or done by the Lord'. And a recently discovered copy of what appears to be a genuine letter from Clement of Alexandria (c. AD 190) also speaks of Peter's teaching as being the basis of Mark's material.

The gospel writer has been identified with the John Mark of Acts, son of Mary, whose house was used by the Jerusalem Christians (*Acts 12:2*). He went with Barnabas (to whom he was related, *Colossians 4:10*) and Paul on their first missionary journey (*Acts 13:4,13*). John Mark, however, left the two Apostles at Perga in Pamphylia and returned home to Jerusalem (*Acts 15:37–40*). No reason is given in *Acts* for this desertion but Paul obviously felt very deeply about it and refused to have John Mark accompany them on the second journey. Paul and Barnabas quarrelled over this and went their separate ways – for a time at least. However, we know from Paul's letters that he and Mark were eventually reconciled as Mark was with him during his imprisonment in Rome (*Colossians 4:10,12 and Philippians 24*). Mark is also associated in the New Testament with Peter. In the first letter of Peter (which is usually considered to bear the authority of Peter then in Rome, even if Silas/Silvanus acted as Peter's amanuensis (*5:12*)), Peter speaks of 'my son Mark' (*5:13*), which endorses the tradition behind the gospel.

The date and place of writing are usually attributed to the mid sixties in Rome, perhaps after the deaths of both Peter and Paul in the first serious persecution of Christians under the Emperor Nero. The scholar John Robinson, however, makes out a convincing case for a much earlier dating of all four gospels.

Understandably people can often be put off by such uncertain conclusions and by the variability of scholarly opinion. But the actual experience of teaching this gospel over a period of 17 years, has convinced me of the vitality and inner experiential veracity of its contents. I like to think that it gives us Peter's assessment of his Master and as such is of great significance for our understanding of Jesus, the man.

Characteristics

It is written in rough and vigorous Greek and this comes across in the English translation, as for example, the use of the word 'straightway' which occurs 41 times. In the first chapters, particularly, there is a sense of urgency with Jesus striding over the countryside teaching and healing, attracting great crowds. It also appears to have been written for Gentiles, for Mark includes three Aramaic phrases of Jesus, which he translates for his readers. He also explains ritual customs (*7:1–23*) and when figs are ripe in Judaea!

2

In some passages there appears to be the immediacy of an **eye witness account** for only in Mark do we find certain details which Matthew and Luke have not considered worthwhile to repeat.

'Now he was in the stern asleep **on a cushion**' and that in the middle of a storm on Lake Galilee *(4:38)*. No wonder his friends were irritated and fearful: 'He ordered them to make the people sit down in groups on the **green** grass, **and they sat down in rows**' *(6:39)*. Only in spring is the grass green in Galilee and the Greek word for rows or ranks, suggests almost the orderly laying out of plants in a garden bed.
'The man's sight began to come back, and he said "I see people – they look like trees, but they are walking about" ' *(8:24)*. This story is found **only** in Mark. The man's words seem a vivid memory of how he recorded the first stage of his sight's restoration. Jesus then completed the cure by a second laying on of hands.
'And **he put his arms round him (the child)**' *(9:36)*, '**And he put his arms** round them (the children), **laid his hands on them**, and blessed them' *(10:16)*. Mark specifically notes Jesus' tenderness with children.
'**As Jesus looked at him,** (a stranger) **his heart warmed to him**' *(10:21)*. This stranger is known by the composite title of the rich young ruler as Matthew records that he was young and rich, Luke that he was a ruler. Mark's contribution is that Jesus responded in love to him.
'They were on the road going up to Jerusalem, and Jesus was leading the way; and the disciples were filled with awe, while those who followed behind were afraid' *(10:32)*. It is **only** from Mark that we know how the disciples felt. What was it about the Master that made him so unapproachable? It would seem that he was wholly absorbed with his own thoughts as he approached the climax of his ministry and indeed of his life. Mark **alone** also tells us the strange story of the young man who witnessed Jesus' arrest *(14:51–52)*, covered only by a linen cloth. He was seized by the soldiers but evaded capture and fled, naked. It is often suggested that this young man was Mark himself, for why otherwise include the incident?

Mark's gospel gives us a **realistic picture of Jesus; a man with intense human emotions**. A comparison with the other two gospels, of the following passages shows how Luke and Matthew have left out the italicised words.
When a leper approached him and said ' "If only you will, you can make me clean". Jesus was *moved to anger*; he stretched out his hand, touched him, and said "I will: be clean" '. Leprosy was regarded as a highly contagious disease, so the man in question was a social outcast and doubted whether Jesus would care to help him. The word 'anger' has been variously translated as 'pity' (RSV) and 'warm indignation' (NEB) *(1:40–45)*.

3

One Sabbath day in the synagogue, there was present a man with a withered arm. To heal such an illness on the Sabbath was a breach of regulations according to scribal tradition. Pharisees in the congregation watched to see if Jesus would cure this man so that they could bring a charge against him. Jesus' reaction – 'looking round at them (the Pharisees) *with anger and sorrow at their obstinate stupidity*, he said to the man, "Stretch out your arm" '. And the man was healed *(3:1–6)*.

'And he was unable to do any miracle there (at Nazareth, his home town), except that he put his hands on a few sick folk and healed them; and *he was astonished* at their want of faith' *(6:6)*.

'Looking up to heaven, he sighed' *(7:34)*. This healing of the deaf mute is found **only** in Mark.

'He *sighed deeply* and said, "Why does this generation ask for a sign?" ' *(8:12)*.

'They (the mothers) brought children for him to touch. The disciples rebuked them, but when Jesus saw it *he was indignant*' *(10:14)*.

'And he took Peter and James and John with him (in the Garden of Gethsemane). *Horror and anguish overwhelmed him*, and he said to them, "My heart is ready to break with grief; stop here and stay awake" ' *(14:33,34)*.

Mark also gives us an unvarnished and honest account of the **disciples' failure to understand Jesus.** They were even perhaps a little irritated with him, when, surrounded by people, he asked 'Who touched my clothes?' They replied, 'You see the crowd pressing round you and yet you ask, "Who touched me?" ' *(5:30,31)*.

They were frankly horrified at Jesus' prediction that he would be rejected and killed. On that occasion, Peter tried to remonstrate with him but Jesus sternly rebuked him: 'You think as men think, not as God thinks' *(8:32,33)*.

They were often confused by his teaching until Jesus explained matters to them: 'privately, to his disciples he explained everything' *(4:34)* and – 'When they were indoors again, the disciples questioned him about this' *(10:10)*. Jesus had occasion to comment on their lack of faith 'Why are you such cowards? Have you no faith even now?' *(4:40)* and on their dullness 'Do you still not understand? Are your minds closed?' *(8:17)*. In the end, they completely let him down. Judas betrayed him *(14:43–45)*, Peter denied him *(14:66–72)* and the others fled at his arrest *(14:54)*. Only the women remained faithful even though powerless *(14:40)*.

Mark's titles for Jesus – Christ, Son of God and Son of Man

At the opening of his gospel, Mark makes a statement of faith: 'The beginning of the gospel (good news) of Jesus Christ the Son of God'. The word Christ or Christos is a literal Greek translation for the Anointed One, in Hebrew, the Messiah. So Christ is a title not a proper name and appears only here.

When a title is needed, Mark uses the word, Messiah, as in *9:41* where Jesus tells his disciples 'whoever gives you a cup of water to drink because you are followers of the Messiah will certainly not go unrewarded'. And again in *15:32*, when Jesus, on the cross, is being mocked by the chief priests and the scribes, 'Let the Messiah, the king of Israel, come down from the cross'.

The actual phrase 'Son of God' appears infrequently in the unfolding narrative. As we have noted, the Gerasene madman called Jesus 'son of the Most High God'. At his trial before the Sanhedrin, Jesus was asked 'Are you the Messiah, the Son of the Blessed One?' to which he replied 'I am,' but he calls himself then and on other occasions 'The Son of Man'. Having seen the manner in which Jesus met his end, the Roman centurion in charge of the soldiers who had crucified him, said 'This man must have been a son of God'.

According to Mark, Jesus had a deep inner experience at his baptism when he was confirmed in his Messianic task. 'And a voice came from heaven: "You are my beloved Son; in you I take delight" ' *(1:11)*. The 'unclean spirits' were said to have recognised Jesus for who he was *(1:34)*. On one occasion, at least, they cried out 'What do you want with us, Jesus of Nazareth? Have you come to destroy us? I know who you are – the Holy One of God' *(1:24)*.

When Jesus had asked his disciples who they thought he was, Peter had declared 'You are the Messiah'. But Jesus had disturbed and alarmed them all at that time by talking of his anticipated suffering, arrest and death *(8:27–33)*. Six days later, he went up a high mountain with his three closest friends and became totally immersed in prayer. His three companions saw him then in an almost translucent, changed light. They believed Elijah and Moses (the two pillars of the Jewish faith) were with him and that a cloud appeared – the Old Testament overshadowing 'Shekinah' of God's presence *(Exodus 13:22; 24:15–16; 40:34)*. From the cloud came a voice: 'This is my beloved Son; listen to him'.

As we have noted, in Jesus' day, God was thought of as dwelling in glory in Heaven, a definite place above the sky and its waters. And those first disciples of Jesus believed that after his death and their experience of his

5

resurrection, he was exalted at God's right hand. They saw their subsequent gift of the Holy Spirit as the external proof of Jesus' exaltation *(cf. Acts 2:32–33* in Peter's first sermon, preached to the astonished crowd at Pentecost/Whitsuntide). Thus the title 'Son of God' was an entirely appropriate appellation for their Master.

In Old Testament usage, 'son(s) of God' can be found with reference to angelic beings and kingship. For example in the Genesis myth *(6:2)* it was 'the sons of the gods (in the RSV – God)' who fell for the beauty of mortal women and in *Job 38:7* 'the sons of God all shouted for joy'. The prophet, speaking on God's behalf, said of the king of Israel: 'I shall be a father to him and he shall be my son' *(2 Samuel 7:14)*. This role is confirmed by the Psalmist *(2:7)*.

The collective use of 'sons of God', meaning the children of God is found in the Revised Standard Version and other translations of the Old Testament *(Hosea 1:10 et al)*. But in the new Revised English Bible, this phrase has been quite rightly altered to express the Fatherhood of God for both men and women as his children. This alteration is clearly seen in *Matthew 6:8*. In the New English Bible, the seventh Beatitude reads 'How blest are the peacemakers; God shall call them his sons'. The REB reads 'Blessed are the peacemakers; they shall be called God's children'. Humanity, according to the Genesis vision, was made in the image of God *(I:27)* and became living beings through the breath of God *(2:7)*. The Quaker phrase 'That of God in everyone' expresses this belief most succinctly.

However, for Mark and the disciples, Jesus was uniquely the Son of God because in him, God fulfilled his promises to his people, and through him, a renewed humanity could find a right relationship with the spiritual source of its being. That this relationship was expressed in terms of fatherhood and sonship is entirely in keeping with the religious heritage of the Jewish faith.

The phrase 'Son of Man' to describe himself is most frequently found in the second gospel and must originate from Jesus himself. It is ambiguous. As we shall see from our study of the gospel, we cannot always be certain in what sense he used it.

It could stand for a representative of humanity as in *Psalm 8:4*:

> What is man that thou art mindful of him,
>> and the son of man that thou dost care for him? *(RSV)*

The REB version brings out the true meaning of the verse:

> What is a frail mortal, that you should be mindful of him,
>> a human being that you should take notice of him?

On the other hand 'Son of Man' could be used as a veiled name for the supernatural figure of the Messiah. In the RSV translation of *Daniel 7 : 13*, we read 'and behold, with the clouds of heaven there came one like a son of man' to whom is given everlasting dominion and kingship over all peoples. (The REB version of this phrase is 'I saw one like a human being coming with the clouds of heaven'.) This figure probably represented the collective faithful remnant of Israel who, having been willing to die rather than renounce their faith, were rewarded by God. For in *Daniel 7 : 18* it is 'the holy ones of the Most High God [who] will receive the kingly power and retain possession of it always, for ever and ever'.

Jesus could have seen himself as this remnant. He was utterly obedient to what he believed to be the will of God, regardless of the cost. But his conception of messianic kingship was of an entirely different order from that visualised by his contemporaries as we shall discuss later.

CHAPTER TWO

Jesus,
a man with extraordinary power

MARK, OF COURSE, PRIMARILY PORTRAYS JESUS as a man with quite extraordinary power. He gives 15 examples of Jesus' healing, eight of which come in the Galilean ministry covered by chapters *1:14* to *7:23*. These healings illustrate how Jesus treated each person he met as an individual with his/her own particular need. He healed the mentally ill by casting out the devil or demons by which they felt themselves possessed *(1:25, 5:8)*. He took Peter's mother-in-law by the hand and helped her to her feet, when she was ill in bed with a fever *(1:31)*. He did the same to the 12-year-old daughter of Jairus, believed to have died before he could reach the house. 'He went in and said "Why this crying and commotion? The child is not dead: she is asleep"; and they laughed at him. After turning everyone out, he took the child's father and mother and his companions into the room where the child was.' Jesus then took hold of her hand and with tender words, he roused her. The girl got up and walked about to the amazement of her parents. Jesus then gave them strict instructions not to talk about it and to give the child something to eat *(5:39–43)*.

He actually touched the leper – breaking ritual and social taboos. He simply spoke to the paralysed man brought to him in dramatic circumstances on a stretcher by four friends, but first he said 'My son, your sins are forgiven'. Afterwards, he told him to pick up his bed and go home *(1:5,10,11)*.
The man with the withered arm was not touched, but told to **stretch** out his arm, which he did in faith and it was restored.

The woman who had haemorrhaged for 12 years had the courageous faith to touch his cloak, thereby breaking the law, since her illness had made her ritually unclean. Mark tells us that Jesus, who was aware that power had gone out of him, sought out the woman in the crowd pressing about him and said to her 'Daughter, your faith has healed you. Go in peace, free from your affliction' *(5:25–34).* But even more striking was the faith of the Gentile woman, a Phoenician of Syria, who begged Jesus to heal her sick daughter ('possessed by an unclean spirit'). She knew quite well the racial barriers which existed between Jews and Gentiles but there was something in Jesus himself, which encouraged her to persist. Jesus never saw the sick child but his response to the mother's wit and courage, brought about a cure *(7:29,30).*

On two occasions when he was in non-Jewish territory, he used sign language. A deaf man, with an impediment in his speech, was taken aside, away from the crowd, Jesus then put his fingers in his ears, spat on his tongue and said 'Be opened' *(7:31–37).* A blind man was also led away out of the village, before Jesus spat on his eyes, laid his hands on him and asked him if he could see anything. Finding the man's sight was partially restored, Jesus completed the cure by laying his hands on him again *(8:22–26).*

That faith was an essential ingredient to healing is brought out further by Jesus' conversation with the father of a very sick boy *(8:14–29).* From the accounts of the boy's symptoms, attributed in those days to demon possession, it would appear that he actually had epilepsy with suicidal tendencies. Jesus had been away up the mountain with his three closest friends. On his return he found a large crowd gathered, including disputing lawyers. The man had brought his son for healing, but the disciples had been unable to cope. Jesus was saddened and angered by the whole situation. The father cried out in his anguish, 'But if it is all possible for you, take pity upon us and help us'. Jesus replied, 'If it is possible! Everything is possible to one who believes'. At once the boy's father cried: 'I believe, help my unbelief'. After a further convulsion, the boy was cured. Afterwards, in reply to the disciples' question about their own inability to heal the boy, Jesus said 'This kind cannot be driven out except by prayer', the implication being that the disciples' prayer life was not yet adequate enough to cope *(9:14–28).*

The last healing found in Mark's gospel is that of blind Bartimaeus, who was sitting on the beggar's pitch outside Jericho when Jesus passed by accompanied by a large crowd of people on their way up to Jerusalem *(10:46–52).* The vivid details are found only in Mark. The cure is again a matter of faith and personal response to Jesus. The fact that the blind man's name was known suggests that he later became a disciple of Jesus.

I do not intend to 'explain' these accounts of healing because we know from our own experience that healing takes place on many levels. Other cultures had tried and proven methods of healing long before Western medical science developed. People are more aware now of the many effective strands in the healing process than they were 50 years ago, as can be seen, for example, in the increasing use of Chinese acupuncture and the popularity of 'alternative' therapies.

Holistic medicine, i.e. treating the whole person, is perhaps an offshoot of the growing knowledge of the interrelation between mental, emotional and physical well being and its reverse. However the triumph of the human spirit over an ailing or fatally sick body teaches us another lesson. The courageous efforts of Pat Seed who helped thousands of people while grappling with her own terminal illness is inspiration indeed and Pat's is not a single example; other men, women and children have lived heroic lives in similar circumstances.

There are other miracles in the gospel story, however, which do need careful examination. They are described as 'nature' miracles because they contravene the laws of nature as we now understand them to exist. It is inevitable that 20th-century people should seek for a scientific explanation of a strange phenomenon and if that is not forthcoming, should either doubt the reliability of the witnesses or suspend judgement until more is known about the workings of our world. This attitude does not conflict with a personal faith in the existence of an ever present creator God. It simply assumes that this divine spirit does not intervene in or break into the basic rhythms or laws on which the universe survives.

In the first of these (4:35–41), Jesus is credited with stilling a violent storm on Lake Galilee when he and his companions were in real danger of drowning. At that time, elemental forces could assume demonic personae in people's minds, not surprisingly for we ourselves know of what terror and devastation hurricanes can bring, even if our meteorologists have mapped out their probable course. Galilee is notorious for its sudden and violent squalls. If Jesus' words are taken literally, they must have been directed at muzzling the forces of the demonic wind and sea. On the other hand, Jesus' effectiveness may be interpreted in another and more familiar guise. It was his friends' tumultuous fear that he calmed, so that they were able to deal with the physical peril until the storm passed as suddenly as it had arisen. Our own human experience will confirm that some people possess a quality of leadership which enables and inspires others to cope with disaster. For Jesus it was enduring faith in the ultimate purposes of the divine creative spirit of Love, whom he called Father, which gave him the strength and resolute will to act. He was surprised that the disciples had not yet learnt this truth. However, they were to do so later. When Paul was journeying to Rome under escort as a prisoner, his faith and courage enabled the ship's company to survive even though the vessel was wrecked off the coast of Malta (Acts 27).

The second story concerned with Galilee, follows the Feeding of the Five Thousand (*Mark 6:45–52*). Jesus left the crowds and went alone up into the hills. The disciples entered the boat to cross the Lake but ran into difficulties in the early hours of the morning. Jesus saw them and went down to the shore to help. Mark records that the disciples had not understood the significance of the feeding of the crowd and were terrified by what they took to be a ghost walking on the water towards them. Jesus spoke to them, 'Take heart! It is I; do not be afraid'. He got into the boat and the troublesome head-wind dropped. The episode is written as if Jesus had the power to walk on water and in Matthew's account (*14:22–36*) Peter attempted to reach Jesus across the sea, but failed. However in John's gospel, the Greek phrase 'walking **on**' could equally be translated '**by**'. Therefore it is quite possible that Jesus walked in the shallows of the Lake towards his friends, and was thus able to get into the boat without rocking it. They could not see distinctly by moonlight where he was and their sense of direction would be confused as they had been blown off course.

Apart from one tribe, Zebulun (*Genesis 50:13*), the ancient Hebrews were not ocean-going peoples. The sea could be a terrifying element for them and the power of the Lord God was manifest in his control of it and other natural forces (*Psalm 107:28–30*):

> Then they cried to the Lord in their trouble,
>   and he delivered them from their distress;
> he made the storm still,
>   and the waves of the sea were hushed.
> Then they were glad because they had quiet,
>   and he brought them to their desired haven.

The whole psalm is a song of praise to the majesty and goodness of God.

It is easy to see that, with hindsight, Jesus' disciples would think of their Master as having a god-like authority and control. Modern readers, however, are bound to ask whether Jesus did have this kind of supernatural quality which is not given to other humans. Even if he did possess such power, would he so have used it?

In another miracle (*6:30–44*) Jesus, by blessing and breaking five loaves and two fishes, is able to feed 5,000 people and to have 12 great basketfuls of food left over. This story is repeated in *8:1–10* when a Gentile crowd of 4,000 were fed from seven loaves. In this case, seven baskets of scraps were collected afterwards. We do not know whether the story of the feeding of the 4,000 is simply a different version of the 5,000 feeding, or quite another occasion as presented by Mark. No doubt the evangelist included it in good faith because for him it clearly showed that what Jesus did for Jews he also did for the Gentiles. Numbers were important images then. Twelve was

11

symbolic of completion. There were 12 tribes of Israel hence the 12 disciples: also 12 months of the year. Seven was the symbol of perfection, there being seven days of the week after the cycle of the moon. Further, of course, the Sabbath was the seventh day. In *Acts 6:1–6*, we read of seven deacons being appointed from the Greek speaking section of the Christian community to help the Apostles in their work. It is not necessary, therefore, to take the numbers in these stories literally as they would speak to the original readers of the gospel of a different kind of truth: these readers would not necessarily share or even understand our concern for meticulous accuracy in these matters. The mysterious feedings, however, have been seen as a symbolic foretaste of the spiritual food available to all believers through the celebration of the Eucharist (the Lord's supper, Holy Communion or Mass). This interpretation is further enhanced by the fourth gospel's account of Jesus' subsequent teaching to the crowd. According to John, the feeding impressed the crowd so much that they wanted to make Jesus king. However, he took evasive action and went up into the hills, only crossing the Lake by night. When people met Jesus later in Capernaum, he offended most of them, including some of his own following, by talking of himself as the **real** Bread of Life (*John 6:1–51*). But to put the whole subject into perspective, it must also be remembered that John omits any reference to Jesus speaking of the bread and wine as his body and blood at their last meal together, as found in the Synoptics, instead he concentrates on Jesus' farewell discourses before his arrest and death, and the fact that he washed the disciples' feet (*John 13*).

A rather different way of looking at the Feedings is to evaluate the effect Jesus had upon the crowd through his teaching and concern for them. When people saw that the disciples were willing to share the little that they had with everybody, they also pooled the food they had inevitably brought with them for a day out in the countryside. As a result of caring and sharing, all were well fed and there were scraps left over. In our present crisis when two thirds of the world go hungry and one third has a surplus, the lesson of mutual support is something that we need desperately to learn. In this interpretation, therefore, the miracle is the change brought about in human nature through Jesus himself. We can all recognise and accept such an influence because we know that other great ones, such as Gandhi and Mother Teresa, have brought about similar changes of mood and heart in the human beings around them.

Although a brief reference has been made to Jesus healing the sick by casting out their demons, further discussion is needed regarding the healing of the Gerasene madman (*Mark 5:1–20*). The man whom Jesus met on the other side of the Lake in the Gentile region of the Ten Towns (Decapolis) was so deranged and wild that he terrorised the neighbourhood. He believed himself to be possessed by a legion of devils. He called Jesus 'Son of the Most High God'. Jesus restored the man to sanity by ordering the expulsion of the devils, apparently into a nearby herd of swine, who then stampeded over the cliff and were drowned. The owners (villagers or townsfolk) of these valuable pigs were naturally very upset over the incident and asked Jesus to leave before he could do any further damage. Jesus did so but instructed the cured 'Legion', who had begged to go with him, to 'Go home to your own people and tell them what the Lord in his mercy has done for you'.

The Jews regarded swine as 'unclean animals' and were forbidden to eat their flesh (*Leviticus 11:7ff*). Jesus' disciples, therefore, would have no problem in associating the death of the pigs with the destruction of the devils but, by contrast, this story faces modern readers with a moral dilemma. We do not attribute mental illness to demon possession whatever the sufferers themselves may think. We do not know what Jesus himself believed but being a man of his time he certainly talked of evil in terms of Satan and his kingdom (*3:20–30*). Even so, would he and could he have deliberately impoverished the resources of the nearby village in such a manner? A further question arises as to our responsibility towards the animal kingdom over which we have such control. Does this story, taken at its face value, assume that Jesus considered that the restoration of one man's sanity was worth a herd of swine? If so does this justify all subsequent experimentation on animals for the benefit of humanity regardless of the cost to the animals?

We can resolve some of our difficulties by trying to visualise the sequence of events. The herdsmen could well have been careless in their supervision of the herd, so taken up were they by the arrival of Jesus and the excitement of his meeting with Legion. The resulting noise and shouting could easily have frightened the pigs so that they ran off in the wrong direction to their death. The herdsmen, not unnaturally, would blame Jesus for this loss and the disciples concurred, although for different reasons.

In reinterpreting all these cases we are simply responding with imagination to the reality of the disciples' experience. If we had been in the boat when the storm blew up, how would we have remembered the incident when the Master saved our lives? How would we have described the awe we felt seeing the figure in the moonlight when we had no idea that the Master might have been there? How would we have interpreted the healing of the madman and the incredible feeding of the two great crowds?

The controversial story of the cursing of the fig tree (*Mark 11:12–14* and *20–21*) also needs to be discussed, although its contextual setting in between the triumphant entry into Jerusalem and the cleansing of the temple is important and will be dealt with later. What we are considering now is the kind of power Jesus had and how Mark presents this power in terms that were appropriate to his own cultural background, if not to ours. Jesus was on the way up to Jerusalem from Bethany, where he had been spending the night. Feeling hungry, he stopped to look at a fig tree on which there was no fruit. It was Passover time, i.e. either the end of March or early April. But in Israel, figs do not ripen until June. Apparently Jesus cursed the tree and the disciples found it dead next morning when they passed.

It is totally out of the character presented to us in the gospels, that Jesus should blight a tree for acting according to its natural growth. In any case did he have this kind of power? It is rather more probable that a withered fig tree stood on the road from Bethany to Jerusalem and became associated with a parable that Jesus told. In the same kind of way I was shown, as a tourist, the Inn of the Good Samaritan, standing by the Jerusalem/Jericho road. Yet the Good Samaritan never existed except in Jesus' imagination. To support the parable theory, we may recall that in Luke's gospel *(13:6–9)*, Jesus recounts a story of a barren fig tree which was given a last chance to be fruitful before it was cut down, symbolic of the religiously unfruitful Israel.
This is surely very reminiscent of the Mark account but makes better sense. Jesus had seen the way in which the religious authorities had allowed the Court of the Gentiles to become a market place. He was to clear the temple area as a strong protest against its misuse. His story of the barren fig tree clearly illustrated his point.

That Jesus had great power over people cannot be in doubt. Whether he had other powers over the natural world, I cannot know, but I refuse to associate him with any influence that is not entirely used in the service of Love. His life and death bear witness to the fact that he saw himself completely as the Servant of the Lord, of Love itself.

CHAPTER THREE

Jesus and controversy

ACCORDING TO ALL THE GOSPELS, Jesus had major, controversial clashes with the Pharisees and their scribes. Mark recounts a number of these incidents and highlights the inner conviction and wisdom with which Jesus dealt with the religious leaders of his day. It is easy to forget that, according to Luke, Jesus was about 30 years old when he began his ministry (*Luke 3:23*), a comparatively young man. Nevertheless, he first astonished the congregation in the Capernaum synagogue on his attendance there after his baptism. 'The people were amazed at his teaching, for, unlike the scribes, he taught with a note of authority' (*1:22*). The scribes would always refer to the immense Oral Tradition of the Rabbis which had accumulated through constant studying of and commentary upon the scriptures.

On Jesus' return to Capernaum, a great crowd collected round the house where he was staying (probably Peter's) to hear him teach (*2:1–12*). It was on this occasion, that he healed the paralysed man and declared 'My son, your sons are forgiven'. This outraged the scribes who were present. Only God could forgive sins. 'How can the fellow talk like that? It is blasphemy!' Jesus further complicated the issue by his awareness of their attitude. 'Is it easier to say . . ."Your sins are forgiven" or to say, "Stand up, take your bed, and walk"? But to convince you that the Son of Man has authority on earth to forgive sins.' He then turned to the man and told him to pick up his bed and go home, which he did. The scribes, therefore, could not deny Jesus' power but what of its source? And for the modern reader in what sense was Jesus using 'Son of Man'? Was he claiming to forgive sins as the Messiah or as the representative of humanity? He taught that the need for forgiveness is fundamental (*11:25*). We must forgive each other and seek forgiveness of God.

After Jesus had called the tax collector, Levi (*2:13–17* – also known as Matthew, *cf. Matthew 9:9–13*) to be his disciple, he had dinner with his friends amongst whom were 'many tax-collectors and sinners'. The job of

15

tax collector went to the highest bidder: there was no fixed rate of tax, so not unnaturally such men were considered dishonest traitors by the rest of the community. The so called irreligious were strongly attracted to Jesus. They were classed as irreligious mainly because they mixed with Gentiles, for the Pharisees believed that the way of religious purity lay in absolute obedience to the Law of God as found in the Torah, the first five books of the Old Testament. The Jewish Torah, of course, contained both ethical and ritual regulations so a person could be contaminated by ritually unclean things as well as people. When the Pharisees and Scribes saw Jesus actually eating with Levi and his friends (perhaps even in Levi's house, although this is not clear from the text) they were frankly horrified and spoke to the disciples about Jesus' wrong behaviour in running such a risk of ritual/spiritual contamination. Jesus answered them in their own coinage, by referring to sin as an infectious disease or illness. 'It is not the healthy who need a doctor, but the sick; I did not come to call the virtuous but sinners.' Jesus also believed that sin was the breaking of the Law of God, but he later summarised the whole Law brilliantly in terms of Love *(12:29,30)*. Sin therefore was the unloving thought, word and action, a universal condition which constantly separates humans from each other and from the source of their being, the divine spirit of Love itself. Jesus, therefore, was not saying he had no time for good people but that the Pharisees had got it all wrong because they also were sinners in the deepest sense even if they did not recognise it.

In another story *(7:1–23)* Jesus made crystal clear his own views on religious purity. For the benefit of his Gentile readers, Mark details the various Traditions of the Elders, for example the strict washings after being in the market place and before eating any food, in case they should eat with defiled hands and thus make themselves religiously impure. Jesus was criticised because his disciples had not observed this custom. The issue was not one of hygiene. Jesus was angered by what he saw as hypocrisy and used *Isaiah 29:13* to point to the very superficial level of worship given to God. 'You neglect the commandment of God, in order to maintain the tradition of men' *(7:8)*.

He then further illustrated his point by using what may have been a specific case. The Aramaic word 'Corban' meaning 'dedicated' was used in the taking of religious vows. Jesus cited an instance where an unscrupulous son had verbally 'dedicated' his money to God, that is set it aside for religious purposes. He had then subsequently refused his aged parents any financial support. 'Anything I have which might have been used for your benefit is Corban' *(v.11)*. The lawyers upheld the keeping of the letter of the law (or vow) even though the son's action went right against the fifth commandment, 'Honour your father and your mother' *(Exodus 20:12)*. 'In this way by your tradition, handed down among you' said Jesus, 'You make God's work null and void. And you do many other things just like that' *(v.13)*.

On a further occasion, Jesus was equally specific. 'Nothing that goes into a person from outside can defile him; no, it is the things that come out of a person that defile him' *(v.15)*. Afterwards, he had to give his disciples a further explanation. Food simply could not defile because it went into the stomach, through the intestines and out into the drain. Of themselves, objects had no power to contaminate either ethically or religiously. It was evil thoughts and false ideas which led to wrong actions. The significant factors were motivation and self-knowledge. Jesus then listed the false attitudes of mind which led to acts of exploitation, murder, ravaging and destruction. Therefore, what is within one's heart and mind is all important since it is this which leads to action. It is the relationship between the inner self and God which makes a person religiously pure.

A fourth controversy with the Scribes and Pharisees also related to their dependence on outward observance rather than inner motivation. The disciples of John Baptist and the Pharisees themselves fasted twice a week as a sign of piety. When they discovered that Jesus did not insist on his own disciples' fasting, they were highly critical *(2:18–22)*. Jesus was not abashed. He went to the root of the matter. Fasting was totally out of place at such a happy time as a wedding. But if something tragic happened to the bridegroom, then his grieving friends would naturally go without food. His hearers would know that some prophetic imagery in the Old Testament depicted God's relationship to his people in terms of husband/bridegroom *(cf. Hosea 2:19)*. Apostasy or infidelity to the one true Lord was then described as adultery or promiscuous behaviour. For the listeners, Jesus' use of 'bridegroom' was open to messianic interpretation. Probably he intuitively knew even at this stage that he was arousing a level of opposition which could lead to his death; hence his reference to 'the bridegroom being taken away'. In the following two short parables he deliberately compared his own teaching to the new wine and cloth which would not mix with the old wineskin and garment. His insights were too radical to be comfortably contained within the outward form of the Judaism of his day. What was true then is also true now, for a faith which concentrates on rite and dogma is not truly of Jesus whether it bears his name or not.

The question of Sabbath Observance was an issue on which Jesus was quite outspoken. One Sabbath, as Jesus and his disciples were walking through a cornfield, his disciples idly plucked the ears of corn (according to Luke they actually rubbed the grain with their fingers – thus 'reaping', which was forbidden). The Pharisees were critical of Jesus for allowing such an infringement of the Sabbath rules. Jesus' answer was twofold. First he referred back to the action of David and his men, who technically broke religious regulations by eating the holy bread which only the priest of the sanctury at Nob was permitted to eat. They were hungry and must have food: their mission was important. Second, 'The sabbath was made for man, not man for the Sabbath: so the Son of Man is lord even of the Sabbath' *(2 : 28)*. The teaching is clear. The needs of people must come first. Human beings are more important than any institution, however sacred. It is totally false when people are sacrificed to maintain established customs even if these were originally of a beneficial nature. There are also subtle undertones in this controversy. Was Jesus claiming to be the messianic son of David? Probably not for this was too political a term for him to use. Was he claiming lordship over Sabbath regulations as Messiah, or as the valid representative of humanity? I think the latter despite the capital letters in the REB text!

On another Sabbath *(3 : 1–6)*, Jesus was in the synagogue where he saw a sick man with a withered arm. The Rabbis taught that only when life was in danger, could healing be permitted on the Sabbath, consequently those present were waiting to see if Jesus would break their tradition. Jesus was aware of their hostility and he challenged them accordingly. How could the Sabbath be truly observed? Surely it was more in keeping with the real nature of Sabbath observance to have the desire to do good rather than evil, to heal rather than to kill? He must have known by this time that his opponents were seriously considering getting rid of him altogether. At the risk of his own life, therefore, Jesus demonstrated both his compassion for the sick man and his belief that people were of greater value than an institution. In fact Mark records that after Jesus had healed the man and the service was over, the Pharisees went outside to plot with the Herodians how to bring about his death. And the Herodians would not be natural allies of the deeply religious and strictly conforming Pharisees who hated Roman overlordship.

By this time, Jesus was apparently being talked about far and wide. His family were concerned for him, even thinking him 'out of his mind'. They resolved to fetch him home. Some Jerusalem lawyers also came to Galilee expressly to question Jesus *(3 : 20–30)*. He was accused of possessing Satanic powers which enabled him to cast out devils. He answered them in kind, as he had done at Levi's party, and he appealed to their common sense. Satan had his kingdom, as they all agreed. But every kingdom and indeed every household needed unity of purpose if it was to survive. How, therefore, could Satan tolerate the kind of rebellion suggested by the accusation?

There was a second flaw in their argument. In order to take a strong man's possessions from him, the intruder must be tougher than the owner. Jesus pointed out that they had not realised the implications of their own remarks: he was able to cast out devils because he had a far greater power than that of Satan.

Jesus was understandably very angry with the Scribes and spoke harsh words about 'the unforgivable sin'. We need to see this phrase squarely in its context for speculation about its exact nature had caused great distress. Faced with Jesus' acts of compassion, the lawyers attributed them to evil. Why were they so blind? Was it not because their arrogant perversity made them unable to recognise goodness in an unfamiliar guise? Their rigidity of outlook and estimation of their value made them unaware of any lack in their religious righteousness or standing with God. To receive forgiveness, we first have to be aware that we need it. We then enter into a reciprocal relationship which involves personal growth and change. Love cannot, does not, impose its will or force upon others that which they are unwilling to receive. It waits in compassionate hope. The sin against the Holy Spirit speaks to us about a tragic condition of human nature where true self knowledge and humility has been lost to be replaced by a self-destructive arrogance. Forgiveness can be given and received only when it is looked for and desired.

One final word must be added about Jesus' controversial relationship with the Pharisees and Scribes. (Matthew and Luke deal with the question in much more detail: *Matthew 23:1–36: Luke 11:37–54*). In Mark's gospel during the last days of Jesus' life, he spoke publicly in the Temple precincts of the scribes' vanity *(12:38–40)*. 'Beware of the scribes, who love to walk up and down in long robes and be greeted respectfully in the streets, to have the chief seats in synagogues and places of honour at feasts.'
But more important to Jesus was the way in which the lawyers exploited defenceless widows, for whom he had great compassion. He was angered by the scribes' hypocrisy and felt the betrayal of their privileged and responsible positions would ensure a corresponding judgement from God. 'Those who eat up the property of widows, while for appearance' sake they say long prayers, will receive a sentence all the more severe.'

From all these examples, it is clear how well Jesus coped with opposition. He had clarity of mind, wit and courage. Further he always used the occasion creatively to teach fundamental truths to those who were receptive enough to receive his wisdom.

CHAPTER FOUR

Jesus the teacher

To the crowds

Mark's record of only four of Jesus' parables is very limited compared with those in Matthew and Luke but it is sufficient to give us a taste of the methods Jesus used. The listening crowds would be familiar with the pictorial way of presenting truth from their knowledge of prophetic and rabbinical sources. Other Eastern sages have long used the story as an effective way of teaching. Scholars differentiate between the parable, which has **one** central point and makes a comparison in phrase or story and the allegory in which **each** point is significant. The familiar parable of the sower *(4:1–9)* has been turned into an allegory by an explanation *(4:3–20)* which may have been added later. The challenging story of the Wicked Tenants *(12:1–12)* is plainly also an allegory full of pointed allusions to Jesus' evaluation of himself and his relationship with the religious leadership.

The parable of the Sower is one of the best known of Jesus' stories. Jesus was sitting in a boat on the lake because of the large crowd 'on the beach right down to the water's edge'. Perhaps he actually saw a farmer scattering his seed on a nearby hillside. In any case the crowd would know precisely what he was talking about. ' "A sower went out to sow. And it happened that as he sowed, some of the seed fell along the footpath; and the birds came and ate it up. Some fell on rocky ground, where it had little soil, and it sprouted quickly because it had not depth of earth; but when the sun rose it was scorched, and as it had no root it withered away. Some fell among the thistles; and the thistles grew up and choked the corn, and it produced no crop. And some of the seed fell into good soil, where it came up and grew and produced a crop; and the yield was thirtyfold, sixtyfold, even a hundredfold." He added, "If you have ears to hear, then hear." '

In Mark's version of the story the seed was the word of God as spoken by Jesus. The soil represented the different responses people made to this

20

message. Some were too hard or shallow or too preoccupied to listen and absorb adequately. Only one in four was credited with a receptiveness that bore abundant fruit in their lives. Jesus was essentially a realist, not a cynic. He knew human nature. From the discussion he had with his disciples afterwards (v.10–12), it was clear that the intuitive, inward reality, which he called 'the secret of the kingdom' was not easily attained. It had to be recognised for what it was and thus greatly desired.

Only Mark tells us Jesus' parable of the farmer sowing his seed which grew 'secretly' to full ripeness and harvesting in a way which the man himself did not understand (4:30–32). We cannot be sure what Jesus meant but it is reasonable to link it with previous sayings. Here perhaps the kingdom is the hidden resource, the spiritual life-force, both within the seed and the soil, which produces growth. It may also have been a comment about the coming spiritual harvest. But the former interpretation is more probable and significant, especially as in the next parable, the Kingdom itself is likened to a mustard seed. 'Small as a grain of mustard seed' was a Jewish proverb, yet from this minute seed could grow a six or eight foot tree/bush. 'The birds of the air' was also a Jewish phrase describing the Gentiles. The coming of the Kingdom began in a very small way with Jesus and his disciples but its growth to include Jew and Gentile was assured.

Parabolic teaching reached people on many levels and invited the listeners to interpret the story as they were able. If an individual did not respond and act upon what he/she had 'heard', i.e. understood in the deepest sense, then they would remain, for the time being at any rate, 'outside' the kingdom. The unresponsive could be likened to those people to whom Isaiah was sent. who heard without hearing and saw without seeing; Jesus used *Isaiah 6:9,10* to illustrate his point. The passage has sometimes caused confusion for if taken literally it would seem that Jesus used the parabolic method deliberately to obscure his message, which is absurd. By quoting from Isaiah, Jesus implied that the majority were not yet awakened and alive to their real needs hence they could not be reached, as yet!

The Pharisees tried another tactic with Jesus by asking him to give some conclusive sign that he was the Messiah (8:11–21). Mark says that they 'tested' him and this word sums it up. They had shown that they thoroughly disapproved of him. They thought of him as a blasphemer, a Law breaker, even as one possessed by the devil. Perhaps it was another group of these men who were doubtful about him, especially the source of his obvious powers. To ask him to prove himself by some overwhelming manifestation was a clever move because it removed from them the responsibility of either an acceptance or a rejection of his ministry. Jesus flatly refused.

It is worth considering this incident in the context of Jesus' teaching methods because it clearly indicates his whole approach. He was not going to win people's allegiance by any apparently supernatural demonstration or contrived 'propaganda'. Jesus quite deliberately decided that messiahship for him meant being the servant of the Lord. He left people free to make up their own minds about him and to follow him out of love and conviction. He gave to each person he met and to the crowds at large, the dignity of making their own choices – hence the parabolic way of imparting truth. Only so could they grow in human maturity and grace. Of course, the unique quality of Jesus' own life, was itself the sign of his special role for those with the perception to understand.

After Jesus had spoken to the Pharisees, he got into the boat with his disciples to make for the other shore. He was obviously angry and took the opportunity to warn his friends of the bad influence exerted by some Pharisees and Herodians, using the metaphor of yeast ('leaven'), to illustrate his point. However his disciples, conscious that they had forgotten to bring any bread with them, quite misunderstood him, which upset him further.

The well known allegory of the Wicked Tenants *(12:1–12)* was a story that Jesus told in the Temple precincts during the last days of his life. Every point has its relevance. The vineyard was a recognisable image for the people of Israel whose owner was God. His hearers would guess that the tenant-farmers left in charge of the vineyard because of the owner's absence, were their religious leaders. As it was the custom to pay rent in kind, Jesus' audience could recognise that what was due to God from Israel as the 'produce from the vineyard' was the right kind of worship and service rendered to God by the quality of their lives. The servants sent to collect the unpaid rent would represent the prophets who had been rejected, beaten and even killed because their message was unacceptable. When the owner finally sent his son (Jesus himself), the tenants killed him and flung his body out of the vineyard thinking that by disposing of the heir, they would then be able to possess the inheritance themselves. 'What will the owner of the vineyard do?' asked Jesus, 'He will come and put the tenants to death and give the vineyard to others.'

Jesus then referred to *Psalm 118:22*: 'The stone which the builders rejected has become the main corner-stone. This is the Lord's doing and it is wonderful in our eyes'. In the Psalm, the corner-stone was Israel, but Jesus must have been applying it to himself. Even if the authorities got rid of him by arrest and death, God would build upon him a real spiritual temple.

Mark tells us 'They (presumably the Sanhedrin) saw that the parable was aimed at them and wanted to arrest him; but they were afraid of the people, so they left him alone and went away'. It would seem that Jesus was warning the Sanhedrin that if they proceeded with their plan to destroy him, disaster would fall upon them. Indeed God would finish his covenant relationship with them and establish it with others, i.e. the Gentiles. Early Christians distinctly believed they were the new Israel, who had entered into a new covenant relationship with God. They saw the destruction of Jerusalem which ended the Jewish revolt in AD 70 as the inevitable result of the Jewish nation's rejection of Jesus.

There is no Sermon on the Mount in Mark. He does, however, give his readers a brief summary of the basic content of Jesus' message *(see p. 36)*. And one of the realistic touches in his gospel is that he does not present Jesus as preaching long sermons on abstract or philosophical themes. Jesus either tells a story or utters short, often enigmatic, statements which need a great deal of thought to interpret adequately. A good example of his epigrammatic style is found in three linked sentences which were probably remembered and grouped together simply because they all contain the word salt:

> Everyone will be salted with fire.
> Salt is good; but if the salt loses its saltness, how will you season it?
> You must have salt within yourselves, and be at peace with one another. *(9:49,50)*

This precious commodity, salt, is an apt symbol of three things: it speaks of preservation or purification by suffering; as seasoning it adds spice to life; in giving and receiving it is symbolic of friendship.

Discipleship

After Peter's acknowledgement that he believed Jesus to be the Messiah, Jesus told his disciples, to their dismay, of his probable suffering and death *(8:27–30)*. Mark records that Jesus then called the people to him and taught them *(8:31 – 9:1)*. The brevity and starkness of the six statements on discipleship make them difficult reading. They must have been very disturbing to those listeners who were hoping for a good time with the coming of the Kingdom.

First: Followers of Jesus must be prepared to suffer and if necessary die ('take up his cross') for their faith.

Second: These paradoxical words about saving and losing underline Jesus' deep penetration into the human situation. If we always grab, giving ourselves priority in everything, we shall become irretrievably diminished as human beings. By contrast, the individual who is nôt deterred from self-giving even though his life is imperilled will find himself enriched and ennobled, for death is not the end.

Third: Of what use is it to gain the whole world and lose our essential self (our integrity; our sense of identity) in the process?

Fourth: What can we give to buy back the true self? How can we regain what we have lost if our actions have constantly negated our very humanity?

Fifth: This statement is couched in the imagery of *Daniel 7:10, 13–14* and specifically refers to the consequences of disloyalty to Jesus. The denial of what we have acknowledged as fundamental truth, will eventually lead to humiliation and shame.

Sixth: This is a difficult saying. 'There are some of those standing here who will not taste death before they have seen the Kingdom of God come with power' *(9:1)*. On the whole, early Christians believed they would not die until they had witnessed the second coming of Jesus. At the start of his mission, Paul also affirmed that the whole historical process would soon be concluded when Jesus the Christ returned in glory. This expectation and the vindication of Christian martyrs was the basis of the book of Revelation written in AD 90s. What could Jesus have meant by the phrase 'The Kingdom come with power'? The Kingdom of God for Jesus was an inner reality, the way of compassionate Love and it was through living it, even unto death, that empowerment came. When Jesus' friends experienced his resurrection from the dead (whatever form that experience may have taken) and consciously received the indwelling Spirit at Pentecost/Whitsuntide, they became radically changed people. There was a quality of inner power generated in them which bewildered their opponents: 'Observing that Peter and John were uneducated laymen, they (the members of the Sanhedrin) were astonished at their boldness (for Peter had answered their interrogation without fear) and took note that they had been companions of Jesus' *(Acts 4:13)*. As we contrast this with Peter's terror-stricken denial that he even knew Jesus *(Mark 14:66–72)* we have to acknowledge Peter's challenging transformation.

If Jesus seemed to be making extravagant claims for himself, we have to remember that he believed he was speaking truth to the human dilemma, as discussed in our opening chapter. If Love is central, then to give oneself in love, loyalty and faith, even though betrayed, is to find oneself. A denial of the capacity to think for others, is the real destroyer. In our own century Gandhi (for whom the Sermon on the Mount was a favourite) was convinced that the perpetrators of violence, evil and wrong-doing were also the sufferers as well as their victims. Jesus' assessment of the nature of Ultimate Reality and our relationship with this reality and each other, was the basis of his own conduct.

In the collection of sayings *(4:21–25)*, which in Mark's gospel followed the parable of the Sower, Jesus seems to have told his disciples that they must broadcast what they have received from him, in essence the 'secret' of the kingdom. A lamp is useless if covered. It must be placed on a lampstand to give maximum light. Hidden things are eventually brought out into the open. The level of the commitment which the disciples give to their relationship will be the measure of what they get out of it 'with something more' added. Furthermore, if people do not use the inborn talents and skills which are given them, they will lose these gifts altogether.

According to Mark, Jesus warned his disciples three times of his inevitable arrest and death but also apparently that he would 'rise again' *(8:20; 9:30–32; 10:32–34)*. Mark bluntly states that the disciples did not understand and on the second occasion 'were afraid to ask'. Perhaps Jesus' terrible rebuke to Peter when he had tried to argue with the Master *(8:33)* had scared them off. We may judge that it is impossible to know what the disciples actually experienced in the resurrection appearance 'three days' after his death *(8:31; 10:34)*. All we know is that the first day of the week (what we now call Sunday) became for them the most sacred day of all because on it the Lord rose from the dead. They may perhaps have used hindsight in remembering or interpreting Jesus' words of 'three days'. Nevertheless it is apparent from Jesus' conduct at his trial that he did expect the reality of his message and person to be vindicated by God. If not, then his understanding of the human situation and his declared truth about the supremacy of Love was a bitter mockery. According to the New Testament witness, this confirmation of Love was given, but only to those who were able to receive it.

Jesus greatly disturbed his friends by this dreadful foreboding, which they did not at all comprehend. They had argued amongst themselves, more than once, about precedence. On the first occasion Jesus said 'If anyone wants to be first, he must make himself last of all and servant of all'. He then took a little child, symbolic of powerless dependence, and put his arm round him 'Whoever receives a child like this in my name, receives me; and whoever receives me, receives not me but the One who sent me' *(9:35–37)*. The significance of this teaching is profound. True greatness lies in service to others. Truly great people have the insight to treat others as people in their own right: especially must the most defenceless in society receive respect. The very idea of classifying people as inferior and superior is totally out of keeping with the divine Love.
Jesus also probably surprised his disciples by acknowledging that many others did his work of compassionate love and healing, without necessarily knowing anything about him personally *(9:38–41)*. How intolerable is this insight to the possessive disciple both of then and now!

Jesus foresaw a dread future for those who endangered others, especially if the victims were children or innocents of any kind (9:42–48). Jesus believed that the total lack of consideration for and recognition of others finally led to the destruction of the real self. In this context, his disciples must be prepared to exercise great self-restraint and control if they were to attain true development: they had to be willing to give up the immediate satisfaction for a longer term good. His graphic imagery of cutting off an offending foot, hand, or eye rather than descend to hell fire, shows us the passionate poet who knew by heart the writings of the prophets. The picture of hell as the place 'where the devouring worm never dies and the fire is never quenched' is a direct quotation from the last verse of the book of Isaiah.

The word translated as 'hell' was literally 'Gehenna', a Greek term for the Jewish Valley of Hinnon. Once a Canaanite sacred site where human sacrifice had taken place, in Jesus' day it was a continually burning rubbish tip which had come to symbolise eternal punishment. The concept of 'eternal torment' is quite alien to Jesus' ministry. He saw that the essential quality of fire is that it totally destroys, so by this symbol, Jesus meant that a person always had the choice between true life in all its creative abundance, or ceasing to exist at all by reason of rejecting these endless opportunities.

Prayer and Love

Mark gives us no Lord's Prayer. On the other hand he shows us quite clearly the importance of prayer in Jesus' life. At the beginning of his ministry, Jesus got up very early and went to a remote spot to pray. Simon Peter and the others later went in search for him. 'Everybody is looking for you,' they said, to which Jesus replied, 'Let us move on to the neighbouring towns, so that I can proclaim my message there as well, for that is what I came to do' (1:35–39). His primary purpose was to teach not heal. In any case he was not inexhaustible. He needed time and solitude for that internal relationship with the source of his being.

The strange story of the transfiguration (9:2–13) shows us the intensity of Jesus' own prayer life. Six days after Jesus had deeply shocked his friends by talking about his almost inevitable arrest and death, he went up a nearby mountain (probably Mount Hermon some 13 miles from Caesarea Philippi) to pray, taking with him Peter, James and John. The three men had a profound experience; watching Jesus at prayer, they saw in him a luminous quality which they could only describe as a transfiguration. It also seemed to them that Jesus was joined by two other figures whom they identified as

Moses and Elijah (the two great pillars of the Jewish faith). Unable to cope with the terrifying wonder of such a situation, Peter blurted out, 'Rabbi, it is good that we are here! Shall we make three shelters, one for you, one for Moses and one for Elijah?' Then they were overshadowed by a cloud, out of which came a voice 'This is my beloved Son; listen to him'. When they looked around, only Jesus was with them.

The story is told from the disciples' viewpoint. The cloud was the Old Testament symbol for the presence of God, the 'shekinah' *(Exodus 13:22; 24:15–16; 40:34)*. The voice confirmed Jesus' messiahship and is very like the inner experience that came to him at his baptism *(cf.1:11)*. The words are similar to those found in Isaiah:

> Here is my servant, whom I uphold,
> my chosen one, in whom I take delight! *(42:1)*

and the promise given to Moses: 'The Lord your God will raise up for you a prophet like me from among your own people; it is to him you must listen' *(Deuteronomy 18:15)*.

We know how the faces of others can be transfigured by deep emotion such as joy; and that the deeply spiritual exercise of inner communion with God can illuminate outward appearance. According to *Exodus 34:29* 'when he (Moses) came down (from Mount Sinai), he did not know that the skin on his face shone because he had been talking with the Lord'. It is not difficult, therefore, to understand how a kind of inner radiance in Jesus, the outcome of his own commitment to his Father, overwhelmed his friends. Perhaps too, a combination of sun and cloud on the mountain top created silhouettes surrounded by circles of light that confused the three men standing a little below. They would of course interpret all they had seen in terms of their own expectations of Jesus. Convincing though this experience was, however, it did not enable Peter to hold fast to its truth at his time of trial.

On another occasion, which in Mark's gospel follows the incident of the shrivelled fig tree, Jesus made extraordinary claims about the effectiveness of faith and prayer: 'Have faith in God. Truly I tell you: if anyone says to this mountain, "Be lifted from your place and hurled into the sea," and has no inward doubts, but believes that what he says will happen, it will be done for him. I tell you that whatever you ask for in prayer, believe that you have received it and it will be yours'. This strong poetic imagery is heady stuff, but Jesus adds a further comment: 'And when you stand praying, if you have a grievance against anyone, forgive him, so that your Father in heaven may forgive you the wrongs you have done' *(11:22–25)*. Therefore what is asked of God is governed by the Law of Love. The key to this law is that we should be willing to give and receive forgiveness. Love should also bring

27

self-knowledge. As we shall discuss later, Jesus was describing what was to him the reality of prayer in terms of interior conversation. Where there is a relationship of love, inordinate and impossible demands are simply not on the agenda.

This is movingly protrayed by the glimpse we get into Jesus' own agony before his arrest and death *(14:26–42)*. After the Last Supper, Jesus and his friends went out of the city across the Kedron Valley to the Mount of Olives, not far from the walls. From all the evidence before him, Jesus obviously knew that the forthcoming events were going to be too much for the disciples. Out of love for them, he warned them that they would probably desert him, using the prophetic verse of Zechariah to describe their isolation – 'Strike the shepherd, and the sheep will be scattered' *(13:7)*. Nevertheless, Jesus attempted to strengthen them by his own faith that he would return to them in Galilee.

When they reached the olive grove called Gethsemane, Jesus knew his only resource was in prayer. He left eight disciples on the fringe of the grove, advising them also to pray and went into the grove with his three closest companions (Judas had already left them at the Supper). 'Horror and anguish overwhelmed him, and he said to them, "My heart is ready to break; stop here and stay awake".' Jesus went a little further, but was still close enough for Peter to hear his words, 'Abba, Father, all things are possible with you; take this cup from me. Yet not my will but yours'. Here was the nub of the matter for Jesus. Love was limitless in its power, but its own nature constrained it to use that power only in the service of others. It was impossible for Love to exploit power for its own advantage.

Jesus found his three friends asleep when he came back to them. 'Stay awake, all of you; and pray that you may be spared the test. The spirit is willing but the flesh is weak.' Twice more he returned to them, to find them asleep. On the last time, hearing the approach of the armed crowd, he concluded, 'Up, let us go! The traitor is upon us'. It is evident from his subsequent courage and resolution that Jesus' own desperate need was met by prayer. He had tapped inexplicable sources of strength to go through with his trial, torture and death: this was indeed vindication of his faith.

In the last days of his life, Jesus spent some time teaching in the Temple area. One day *(12:41–44)* as he was sitting opposite to the Temple Treasury, in the Court of Gentiles, he saw a very poor widow. It was the custom to declare the amount of your gift as you put it into one of the 13 great trumpet boxes. The rich gave of their plenty, but this woman gave all she had. In Jesus' estimation her gift therefore was priceless. How he knew her circumstances is not clear, but we sense his sympathy and awareness of other's needs. By commonsense standards, her gift was not wise for how would she be able to buy food for tomorrow? We cannot answer this question, but we can see that for Jesus, the motive behind the gift was all important: 'Truly I tell you: this poor widow has given more than all those giving to the treasury; for the others who had given had more than enough, but she, with less than enough, has given all that she had to live on'.

The second incident occurred in the house of Simon the leper at Bethany *(14:3–9)*. 'As he sat at table, a woman came in carrying a bottle of very costly perfume, pure oil of nard. She broke it open and poured the oil over his head.' Some of those present were indignant at what they considered to be waste, feeling the ointment could have been sold and the proceeds given to the poor. But Jesus reacted quite differently. He praised the woman for her costly and intuitive act of love. It would seem that she had sensed his imminent death. In this special situation, it was not valid to contrast her outpouring of grieving love with the permanent needs of the poor.
We are separated from this particular story by a cultural gap. In Jesus' day, the anointing of the body for burial was customary, and oil was widely used to compensate for the very hot, dry climate. The cultural details can therefore be readily understood and should not disturb the modern reader; the story's challenge to us lies in love's capacity for total giving.

Mark follows this story with a stark contrast – the details of Judas' treachery. For the price of a good sum of money, he told the Sanhedrin where and when Jesus could be arrested privately without causing too much disturbance. We simply do not know why Judas did this, although all kinds of possible motives have been suggested. According to *Matthew (27:3–10)*, he suffered terrible remorse afterwards and tried unsuccessfully to 'buy Jesus back'. Later he committed suicide.

CHAPTER FIVE

Questions and Answers

MARK OFTEN PORTRAYS JESUS in the question and answer situation which was a familiar aspect of rabbinical teaching. According to this gospel, seven major questions, some of which were hostile, were put to Jesus in the latter part of his ministry, the last and most important of all forming part of his cross-examination at his trial. A great deal of teaching and comment takes place indirectly through question and answer as Jesus used every opportunity, including his opponents' attacks, to speak to people's needs.

The **first** question referred to marriage and divorce. While travelling through Judaea and Transjordan to keep Passover at Jerusalem, Jesus was asked, probably by some Pharisees, whether it was lawful for a man to divorce his wife *(10:1–12)*. Current rabbinical debate on this topic involved diverse interpretations of *Deuteronomy 24:1–4* which stated that a man could give his wife a certificate of divorce if he had found 'something offensive in her'. Rabbi Shammai said this specifically meant sexual infidelity. Rabbi Hillel applied it much more widely, saying it could include for example, failure in domestic duties. In any case, according to the law, the woman had no rights in the matter at all.

Jesus was not interested in legal wrangling but in discovering any aspect of truth which lay behind the precepts of the law. He dismissed the Deuteronomic instruction (which he of course attributed to Moses) as being a concession to human weakness and went back to Genesis, using the two accounts of Creation *(1:27* and *2:24)* to illustrate his concept of true marriage. Men and women were created by God. In sexual intercourse, 'they are no longer two individuals: they are one flesh. Therefore what God has joined together, man must not separate' *(10:1–9)*.

To attribute dogma to Jesus is to fall into the trap of literalism. He never legislated and he did not do so here. He affirmed that marriage was a **mutual** commitment of love and fidelity: an act of **loving** union – actually what **God** had joined. Therefore blessing and joy sprang naturally from such a relationship and it must not be disrupted by the designs of others. Incidentally, it is interesting to note that he did not say that the purpose of marriage was procreation, although it is clear that he loved and valued children.

In private, the disciples questioned him further. They were disturbed to find Jesus' ideas so radical for he made it clear that the Mosaic regulations were unfair to women. Jewish law stated that adultery was not an offence against a man's wife, but only against the husband of the other woman with whom the adulterer had had sexual intercourse. On the other hand Roman law allowed a wealthy woman to divorce her husband. This was why Herodias' second marriage to Herod Antipas was strongly condemned as adulterous by John Baptist.

Jesus confirmed that he regarded men and women as equals in the marriage relationship. A man who divorced his wife and married another, committed adultery against his first wife and vice versa. Jesus was not redefining adultery as opposed to fornication. The former has always been regarded in a different light because it broke the serious commitment involved in marriage. Nor did Jesus say that divorce was always wrong. He stated what he believed to be the principle behind a sexual union of two committed people, treating men and women as equals at a time when women were regarded as distinctly inferior. In *Matthew's gospel (6:27,28)* we are told that he strongly condemned lust. He was always concerned with motivation and a fresh interpretation of the law in terms of human experience.

The **second** question had to do with priorities *(10:17–30)*. A stranger approached Jesus to ask what he must do to win eternal life. After challenging the young man about his conventional form of greeting, Jesus discovered that he was indeed an upright Jew who had kept all the commandments since youth. Jesus was compassionate but deeply perceptive. He discerned that the stranger's riches were his unconscious priority, so he invited him to 'Go, sell everything you have, and give it to the poor, and you will have treasure in heaven; then come and follow me'. The man was unable to accept this invitation and went sadly away. Obviously Jesus felt this rejection deeply and he warned his disciples that the corrupting nature of riches could prevent entry into the kingdom. Having experienced poverty themselves, the disciples were astonished. They believed the rich had fewer temptations than the poor. If the wealthy found entry to the kingdom difficult, what hope was there for others? Jesus knew that the inner reality of the kingdom of God depended on quite other qualities than the human values of privilege, endowment or worldly need.

Impulsively, Peter asked Jesus about the disciples' own chances of earning eternal life, as they had left everything to follow him. Jesus

31

reassured them. There was a basic law of giving and receiving which operated at the deepest level of human experience even if it was not always recognised. Having given up so much for Jesus, the disciples would indeed receive back a hundred fold through the spiritual family/community which Jesus was creating. Even though persecution was inevitable, they could be sure of their inheritance, eternal life being a present reality as well as a future hope. Again, Jesus was not making laws. He saw that one particular rich man needed to give up his wealth; he did not say that all wealth should be abolished. On another occasion *(Luke 19:1–10)* he advised the honest and responsible use of wealth but did not tell the owner to give it away.

Although all but one of the remaining questions were definitely hostile, Jesus used them creatively to teach important lessons, not least that his enemies could not get the better of him in debating trickery. He had made a triumphal entry into Jerusalem and the next day had cleared dishonest practitioners and practices out of the Temple precincts. The Sanhedrin were not unnaturally appalled by his actions and demanded to know his authority *(11:27–33)*. They frankly hoped he would make some damaging admission for which they could legitimately arrest him. But instead of answering directly, Jesus counter-questioned them about their attitude to John Baptist: Was he god-inspired or not? The Sanhedrin were faced with a dilemma; John Baptist who had initially witnessed to Jesus as the coming Messiah, had been gladly received by ordinary people and recognised by them as a great prophet. The Sanhedrin's popularity was at risk. So they refused to commit themselves and their question remained unanswered by Jesus.

A mixed group of Pharisees and Herodians asked Jesus a question about tribute money *(12:13–17)*. When Archelaus, son of Herod the Great, had been deposed in AD 6, he was replaced by Roman rule. As a direct consequence, a Roman tax in silver denari, stamped with the Emperor's image, was imposed upon the area's inhabitants. This tax was bitterly resented by the Jews, especially as apparently it went into the Emperor's private purse. Pharisees and Herodians were not easy bedfellows as they represented different attitudes to Roman overlordship. By combining their attack it seemed they had caught Jesus in a trap. If he agreed the tax was lawful, the Pharisees would denounce him as disloyal to Jewish independent sovereignty. If he said unlawful, the Herodians would report him as a dangerous political agitator. However, Jesus was equal to the occasion. He requested a silver piece and asked whose image and inscription was upon it. When told it was Caesar's, he said 'Pay Caesar what belongs to Caesar and God what belongs to God'. The latter phrase referred directly to the Genesis statement *(1:26,27)* that humanity is made in the image of God.

As citizens of any organised community, we have an obligation to support society's legitimate claims, which may include taxation. However, our greater and more important offering is to the Creator in whose image we have been made.

Mark's gospel only once refers directly to the Sadducees. Their question to Jesus *(12:18–27)* based on *Deuteronomy 25:5–10* was about life after death. If a man died childless it was his brother's duty to marry the widow. The first son born of this second marriage 'will perpetuate the dead man's name so that it may not be blotted out from Israel'. The traditional belief, therefore, was that only through his descendants could a dead man live on. Their question – if one woman had seven brothers as husbands, one after another, but remained childless whose wife was she at the resurrection? – was probably aimed at ridiculing Jesus. But they had misjudged their man. 'How far you are from the truth!' he replied. 'You know neither the scriptures nor the power of God.' There was indeed a life after death but one in which the physical body was changed into a spiritual body 'like the angels in heaven'. The procreative side of marriage was therefore unnecessary. To substantiate his belief in the resurrection of the dead, Jesus then quoted from the Pentateuch which the Sadducees so revered. In *Exodus 3:6*, the call of Moses, God declared himself **to be** the God of the Patriarchs. 'He is not the God of the dead, but of the living.' The Patriarchs, therefore, had a continuing relationship with God even though they had lived centuries before Moses.

One of the great debates amongst the Rabbis of Jesus' day, was whether the ritual regulations had the same importance as the ethical and whether therefore the law, which was assessed as having 613 commandments, should be shortened. The question by the Scribe, therefore, asking Jesus *(12:28–34)* which was the chief commandment was probably put in all sincerity. Jesus certainly answered it with a definitive statement of faith. In Luke's gospel the Scribe then said 'who is my neighbour?' While Jesus did not answer directly, after he had told the story of the Good Samaritan, he asked the Scribe to answer his own question – a perfect example of Jesus' teaching methods.

The final question was asked of Jesus at his trial before the Sanhedrin *(14:53–65)*. When all the accusations against Jesus had failed because the witnesses could not agree amongst themselves, the High Priest intervened. He was astonished at Jesus' silence under cross-examination. According to Matthew's gospel, he put Jesus on oath to answer the question (which Mark faithfully reports) 'Are you the Messiah, the Son of the Blessed One?' 'I am,' said Jesus; 'and you will see the Son of Man seated at the right hand of the Almighty and coming with clouds of heaven.' Jesus' imagery reflected

Daniel 7:13 'and I saw one like a human being ("son of man" in the RSV) coming with the clouds of heaven' also *Psalm 110:1* 'This is the Lord's oracle to my lord: "Sit at my right hand"'. Jesus' admission was enough for the Court. The High Priest tore his clothes (a sign of the death sentence) and said 'Do we need further witnesses? You have heard this blasphemy. What is your decision?' Their judgement on Jesus' guilt was unanimous and they condemned him to death.

We need to try to understand both the claim that Jesus made and its implications. That he chose to describe himself in terms of Daniel's 'son of man' figure was a profound comment on his concept of messiahship and its significance is brought out by the REB translation. Jesus saw himself as the representative or even the remnant of the faithful Israel, which in turn regarded itself, through its prophetic vision, as the mediator or interpreter of one true living God to the whole of humanity. Jesus' pictorial reference to the Davidic poetic phrase 'sitting at God's right hand', had surely nothing to do with earthly power and glory. It expressed his inner conviction that if he was faithful to his message of truth about the human situation, he would be vindicated in the end by God, the Ultimate Reality of all things.

34

CHAPTER SIX

The special nature of Jesus' vocation

HOW DID JESUS' SEE HIS VOCATION? Our first insight into this question comes when Jesus came to be baptised by John, thereby identifying himself with John's work of creating a new Israel. At his baptism, he had a profound experience which confirmed him in his messianic role. He must have told his disciples something of this later in his ministry, for Mark indicates that the vision and the voice came to Jesus alone.

We know how Jesus expressed himself in graphic images: 'eating up' the property of widows *(Mark 12:40)* is but one small example! But we also need to appreciate how much Jesus expressed his ideas in poetic symbols, metaphors and form: he was in fact a poet. (In his book **The Poetry of our Lord**, Dr. C. F. Burney demonstrated, by translating the sayings of Jesus from the written Greek into the original Aramaic which Jesus would have spoken, that the principles of Hebrew poetry applied to his form of teaching. Hebrew poetry, as opposed to English, emphasises sense-parallelism rather than rhyme. Four kinds of sense parallelism are found in Old Testament poetry.)

We must bear all this in mind, when we look at the significance of the words used to describe Jesus' baptism. 'As he was coming up out of the water, he saw the heavens break open and the Spirit descend on him, like a dove. And a voice came from heaven: "You are my beloved son, in you I take delight"' *(1:10,11)*.

The Jews thought of heaven as a definite place, where God dwelt in glory; it is idle to speculate whether or not Jesus himself visualised the eternal spirit as 'up there'. He certainly could have used these terms in talking about his inner experience. The descent of the Spirit, described as a dove, indicated the nature of the visitation. In Old Testament thought, when the Spirit of the Lord came upon the prophets to give them insight and power, it often led to denunciation of the iniquities of a faithless people. By contrast, the dove, however, was a well-loved and gentle creature, a not uncommon image for the Spirit amongst the Rabbis of Jesus' time. As the Genesis Flood myth indicated, it was also a symbol of peace, showing when God's judgement had abated and harmony was restored. The confirmation of his messiahship would naturally come to Jesus in familiar and well known words.

' "You are my son," he said to me; "this day I become your father" ' (*Psalm 2:7*). 'Here is my servant, whom I uphold, my chosen one, in whom I take delight!' (*Isaiah 42:1*).

Jesus understood his role, therefore, in terms both of Son of God, probably in a unique sense, and also as the servant of the Lord. These images are, of course, complementary to, not contradictory of, each other.

After his baptism, Jesus went into the wilderness to think through what kind of a messiah he was going to be. It might be considered a strange omission in Mark that he gives us no details of this personal conflict. However, an account of the temptations is found in both Matthew and Luke and forms part of what could have been the first written record of Jesus' sayings, as opposed to the narrative of his life. These collected 'Sayings' were obviously not known to Mark in that form, as they are not included in his gospel. We shall see in later discussion on Matthew that the Temptations confirm Mark's picture of Jesus as pre-eminently the servant of the Lord. During the period when Jesus was away in the wilderness, John Baptist was imprisoned by Herod Antipas, and later killed through the machinations of Herod's second wife, Herodias.

On Jesus' return to Galilee, he began his ministry with the proclamation, 'The time has arrived; the Kingdom of God is upon you. Repent, and believe in the gospel' (*1:14,15*). This is dramatic stuff, in keeping with a long line of prophetic utterances. Mark's opening verses recall the words of Isaiah (*40:3*) and Malachi – one of the post-exilic prophets – (*3:1; 4:5,6*), to show that John Baptist was the anticipated herald of the coming day of the Lord which was, above all else, a day of judgement. Jesus saw God's kingdom and indeed judgement with a different perspective from John Baptist, but he did declare that the long time of waiting through the preceding centuries was now over, for God's kingdom was 'at hand' or in process of realisation. He was much misunderstood by his contemporaries and even his disciples in the matter of the kingdom, just as he had been by succeeding generations of Christians. For his contemporaries, the kingdom of God had geographical, political, racial and even social implications. Despite previous prophetic warnings to the contrary, many ordinary people looked for the 'coming of the kingdom' in the hope of seeing God's universal vindication of his chosen people after years of political instability and overshadowing by more powerful states.

Later generations of Christians, especially under the threat of persecution and death for their faith, thought of the kingdom as life hereafter. In today's world, kingship and kingdom are alien concepts for many people. The words speak of imposed hierarchical structures that have brought oppression and suffering and ought therefore to be abandoned. For Jesus, however, the kingdom was the rule or reign of God, of Love itself, in people's minds, hearts and lives. It was in truth a state of being, a here and now which if entered into would prepare one for whatever lay ahead in the future.

Jesus' two requirements for entry into the kingdom show that it is an inner reality. Repentance involves facing up to present inadequacies and failures in the whole of life and being willing to change direction. Believing in the gospel (the good news Jesus brought), is simply seeing the truth and personal application of his message. Acceptance of this means that we put love first. This faith renews and empowers us to seek for deeply fulfilling goals.

We cannot doubt that Jesus was a man of action. He travelled about Galilee preaching and healing. He called his first four disciples from their daily work at the lakeside. Peter and his brother Andrew, the brothers James and John were all fishermen (1:14-19). It is easy to minimise the charisma of Jesus because of our long association with the gospel story, but the fact that these and other men simply left their homes and jobs to follow him should not be underestimated. Then, from amongst his followers, he selected 12 men who were to be his constant companions (3:13–19). Twelve, of course was symbolic of the 12 ancient tribes of Israel, and Jesus himself probably believed he was creating a new people of God on these simple foundations. Judas Iscariot (meaning 'man of Kerioth') was the only non-Galilean amongst them, so from the beginning he may have felt isolated. Also amongst the 12 was Simon, the Zealot. Jesus was condemned to death by Pontius Pilate on a charge of treason as if he had been a Zealot himself. But it is clear from his ministry, that although he was vey radical in his outlook it would be a great mistake to confuse his message with teaching on the value of physical violence or armed resistance of any kind: quite the contrary.

After he had been with his disciples for a little time, he sent them out on a mission, to see how they would get on without him (6:7–13). Mark places this event after Jesus had been turned down by people in his own town of Nazareth. They could not credit that someone whom they had known as the local carpenter, whose mother, brothers and sisters were there with them, could be a prophet. 'Where does he got it from? Where is this wisdom he has been given?' Jesus remarked, 'A prophet never lacks honour except in

37

his home town, among his relations and his own family.' This lack of response may have influenced the timing of the disciples' mission. Jesus gave the 12 precise instructions what to take and how to act. Their power to preach, heal and exorcise evil spirits was to be used in his name. They were to be messengers of the kingdom. From the way people subsequently talked about Jesus, the mission was obviously successful.

It was Jesus' vocation to awaken people to the primacy of the kingdom, therefore the kingdom in all its aspects was the paramount theme in his parabolic teaching. Certain incidents in Mark also bring out its priority. When his family came to bring him home, having heard wild rumours of his activities and apparently not understanding the nature of his mission, Jesus rejected their concern. He was so deeply committed to the realisation of the kingdom that he declared his true family consisted of those who were obedient to the will of God. This seemingly harsh statement of his priorities did not mean that Jesus did not love his relatives or that he was permanently alienated from his family; on the contrary, we know from other sources, that his mother, Mary, was with him when he died and one of his dying concerns was for her support (*John 19:26,27*). His brother, James, became head of the Jerusalem church (*Acts 15:13*), being martyred for his faith in AD 62. (*Josephus' Antiquities: xx.200* – published ca. AD 93–4).

One day the disciples had made Jesus angry by trying to prevent mothers from approaching Jesus to ask for his blessing on their children (*10:13–16*). 'Let the children come to me: do not try to stop them: for the kingdom of God belongs to such as these. Truly I tell you: whoever does not accept the kingdom of God like a child will never enter it.' Enigmatically Jesus does not elaborate on the special childlike quality which an adult needs in order to enter the kingdom. Quite obviously it is **not** innocence! One essential quality in a child is its openness, its readiness to learn and to receive. This is the exact opposite to the arrogant pride, rigidity and self-centredness which can make adults unaware of their needs. The closed minds and hearts of some of the Pharisees and scribes show how the kingdom, as Jesus presented it, simply did not exist for them at all.

On their way up to Jerusalem for the Passover, Jesus received a request from the brothers, James and John (*10:32–45*), which must have greatly saddened him. If James and John did not understand the nature of his kingdom, how much more incomprehensible was it to others? The sons of Zebedee asked their Master for a favour, 'Allow us to sit with you in your glory, one at your right hand and the other at your left', Jesus replied that they did not understand what they were asking:

Can you drink the cup that I drink,
Or be baptised with the baptism I am baptised with?

His words refer to drinking the cup of wrath (*Isaiah 51:17*) and the baptism of deep waters (*Ps. 42:7; 69:2,15*). This use of Old Testament metaphors to describe the bitter suffering and death he anticipated, emphasises the poetic form (i.e. synthetic parallelism) of his thought. The brothers took his imagery literally and Jesus accepted that they had a genuine desire to follow him. However, the chief places in the kingdom were not in his gift.

The rest of the disciples were very angry when they heard of this conversation but Jesus used the incident to emphasise that greatness in his kingdom was of a different order from that found in the exercise of worldly dominion and authority. It involved perception and service. He himself came not to be served but to serve. Then, for the first time, Jesus gave a reason why he felt he must go through with his service even if it led to his death for he had come 'to give his life as a ransom for many'. In the New Testament era a ransom was the purchase price to release someone from slavery. In what sense did Jesus believe that his death could free humanity – for the 'many' must include both Jew and Gentile? Jesus would be well versed in the Servant Songs of Isaiah (*42:1–4; 49:1–6; 50:4–9; 52:13 – 53:12*) where the vicarious suffering of the faithful servant of the Lord brought salvation to all. Isaiah's explicit monotheism was not simply for the Jews but involved the whole world.

Could Jesus really have believed that the divine being whom he called 'Father' could demand the price of his life as a restitution for others' sins? This transactional language has had long usage in Christian circles, but the idea runs counter to everything Jesus did and said. We need to re-examine the significance of his life and faith. Looking at his ministry, we can see that Jesus was not prepared to give up his teaching. He felt compelled to declare what he considered to be the truth about humanity's search for God or Ultimate Reality, about the purpose of life and its fulfilment, about relationships in family and community. He realised that fidelity to his commitment was leading inevitably to his death, but believed that through this witness, he would show the supreme importance of his convictions. He also trusted that he would be vindicated by the divine Spirit of creative truth and love whom he served. Further, by living out his principle of love to the ultimate, he would act as a great liberating and creative force which would free others from their bondage of blinding self-regard and mistaken objectives.

Jesus eventually left Galilee, going first into the region of Syrophoenicia and thence to Decapolis. Returning to Jewish territory, he travelled to Bethsaida and into the area of Caesarea Philippi. Jesus then moved south. His ministry in the north and Galilee was over (*9:30–32*). Mark portrays him as only once going up to Jerusalem for the Passover but he must have visited Jerusalem several times. We know that he had friends both in Bethany and in a neighbouring village since he had obviously arranged in advance to borrow a young colt for his entry into Jerusalem. Mark had previously shown Jesus at pains to avoid public acclamation of his messiahship, but he tells us that Jesus rode in triumph into the city of Jerusalem *(11:1–11)*. It is not difficult to see why Jesus now felt he must so proclaim himself. But he had to show his people how different his ideas were from their own. The symbolism of his triumphal entry is therefore important. He rode on an untried colt, which made it suitable for sacred purposes. It was a donkey not a horse, therefore he came in peace. He was greeted joyously by the crowds, some of whom cried 'Blessed is the kingdom of our father David, which is coming!' Jesus carefully led the people into the Temple area, within reach of the Roman garrison which would be fully manned at Passover time, and they then peacefully went home. Jesus himself (according to Mark) 'looked round at everything' and then went out to Bethany where he was staying for the Passover period.

On the next day, Jesus cleansed the temple *(11:15–18)* – a truly remarkable act of authority! The Temple buildings consisted of courtyards. First came the Court of Gentiles, then the separate Courts for Jewish women and the Court of Israel (for Jewish men) finally the Court of the Priests and the Holy Place where the altar of sacrifice stood. At the heart of the Temple, was the Holy of Holies, entered only once a year by the High Priest on the Day of Atonement. Sacrifices were offered daily. The market for the sale of sacrificial animals and food stood in the Court of the Gentiles and had to be paid for in Jewish money. Considerable profit was made by the exploitation of pilgrims, to the benefit not only of the traders but the Sadducees who controlled the Temple area. Jesus was outraged by the abuse of the Temple as a place of worship. He swept the Gentile Courtyard clear of the market and stopped it being used as a thoroughfare. 'Does not scripture say, "My house shall be called a house of prayer for all nations"? *(Isaiah 56:7)*. But you have made it a robbers' cave' *(Jeremiah 7:11)*. Jesus' condemnation of the materialistic, narrow nationalism of the Jewish leaders showed clearly his concern for all people, Jew and Gentile alike.

Mark presents the Last Supper as a Passover feast *(14:17–25)*. It may have been held in the house of Mary, mother of John Mark. However the text does not say so because it emphasises that Jesus made sure Judas did not know beforehand where it was to be . During the supper, Jesus said, 'Truly, I tell you: one of you will betray me – one who is eating with me'. This stark announcement deeply dismayed his disciples and they questioned him: 'Surely you do not mean me?' Jesus then answered; 'It is one of the Twelve who is dipping into the bowl with me. The Son of Man is going the way

40

appointed for him in the scriptures; but alas for that man by whom the Son of Man is betrayed! It would be better for that man if he had never been born.'

If taken literally, Jesus' words smack of predestination – a doctrine which I believe to be totally unacceptable to the picture Jesus has given of God/Love. We have seen how steeped he was in his people's ancient scriptures. He often used their words to express his own thoughts. Given the opposition to him, it was inevitable that he would die and it would be natural for Jesus to see his own death in terms of *Isaiah 53*, describing the acute suffering of the Servant of the Lord.

Jesus' words at supper constituted a last appeal of love to Judas for Judas' own sake, as if he were saying – I know what you have in mind. Think again before you do it. You will so bitterly regret your betrayal. When this appeal failed, Jesus did not prevent Judas from leaving the room, as he could easily have done. His love was such that he left him free to act.

It is hard for us to look freshly at Jesus' words about his body and blood after centuries of intense sacramental usage. Although his language would have been very shattering to his companions, it would be less strange than to us because he was using the accepted terms for the sacrificial system and especially the Passover rituals. The earliest Old Testament account of this festival is in *Exodus (12:1–28)*. The blood of the slain male yearling lamb or kid was smeared on the two doorposts of every Israelite household as a sign of deliverance. For the Lord passed through Egypt that night in judgement, and every first born man and beast died unless it was within the shelter of a marked household. Later, when Moses brought the Israelites out of Egypt to Mount Sinai, they entered into a covenant relationship with their God. The actual ceremony is described in *Exodus 24:1–8* when the sprinkling of the blood of the sacrificed animal was used as a symbol binding Israel to God. These ancient stories are separated from us by 3,000 years. In many respects they are alien to our thinking but it is not surprising that Jesus used the religious terminology of his race even though his beliefs in the nature of divinity were radically different.

Before the Exodus story and Mosaic Covenant, Genesis gives us an earlier covenant which was made with Noah after the Flood *(Genesis 9:1–7)*. This forbade humanity to eat the blood of an animal because the blood contained the life principle and was therefore sacred to God. In the first of the Genesis creation myths, humanity was made in God's image *(1:27)*. In the second *(2:7)* man was made a living creature by God's breath. In both stories, therefore, humanity has that of God within, i.e. the spirit. Thus body, soul (the life principle) and spirit are the total human being.

By offering his body and blood (symbolised in the bread and wine) in

41

ancient ritualistic and sacrificial terms, Jesus uttered the belief that through giving himself, he would establish a new covenant, a new relationship between humanity and God. Since Jesus realised that God was Love, his words cannot imply that Jesus actually thought himself a sacrificial victim or believed his death a restitution for people's sins. Love itself could not contemplate such a bargain.

He must have meant that his willingness to die for what he believed to be the truth about God and human nature, would make him a liberating force to all. He was not only willing to die, but by his conduct and teaching, he had demonstrated the power of a sacrificial love that is prepared to give everything for the sake of others. His steadfast belief in love of God and love of neighbour as all important, would be the basis of a new community with Love/God at its centre. By asking his friends to share in his self-offering, through accepting the bread and wine, he was in fact inaugurating this new Covenant. Finally, Jesus made a solemn vow: 'Truly I tell you: never again shall I drink from the fruit of the vine until that day when I drink it new in the kingdom of God'. The purpose of the vow is not clear, but the words contain a future promise of joy and newness of life.

CHAPTER SEVEN

The last days

THE SANHEDRIN POSSESSED THE POWER TO ARREST. Judas led an armed band
of men to Gethsemane and identified Jesus from amongst the other men by
giving him the kiss with which a disciple might greet his master *(14:43–52)*.
Jesus offered no resistance but one of his followers (Peter, according to
John) drew a sword to make a fight of it and cut off the ear of the High
Priest's servant. Jesus commented drily on the swords and cudgels with
which the men were armed for, 'Day after day I have been among you
teaching in the temple and you did not lay hands on me'. Nevertheless he
saw his arrest as following the pattern of the scriptures; he may have had
Isaiah 53 in mind, or possibly *Psalm 41:9*: 'Even the friend whom I trusted,
who ate at my table, exults over my misfortune'.
Jesus had two trials. Before the Jewish authorities he was found guilty of
blasphemy, but apparently only the Roman governor had the power to
execute the death sentence at that period, so it was necessary for Jesus to
appear before Pontius Pilate too. Pilate would not be interested in a charge
of blasphemy, so Jesus had to be convicted of treason. When asked by Pilate
if he was the King of the Jews, Jesus replied 'The words are yours',
probably meaning 'I would not express it like that'. Much to Pilate's
astonishment Jesus made no further answer to any of the accusations
brought against him.
According to Mark (although there is no external evidence substantiating
his claim), on a great occasion like the Passover, it was customary for the
Roman governor to make some concession to his subject people, by
releasing a political prisoner *(15:1–21)*. Mark assumes that his readers
know already about some nationalist revolt involving a man called
Barabbas. Pilate 'knew that it was out of malice that Jesus had been handed
over to him'. In an attempt to save Jesus, Pilate therefore asked the crowd
whether he should release 'the king of the Jews', but they clamoured for the
release of Barabbas and the crucifixion of Jesus. Pilate then had Jesus
flogged, preliminary to his execution.

43

That a crowd could one day greet Jesus with cries of 'Hosanna' and less than a week later demand his death is not surprising. We must realise that few of Jesus' supporters, whether Galilean or not, would have had any knowledge of what was happening. This was plainly the strategy of the authorities and why they enlisted Judas' help. In addition, the crowd present before Pilate had been 'incited' to give the right response not only by the chief priests but surely also by other opponents, including the temple merchants. It could also be said that Jesus had not come up to popular expectations.

A Roman flogging was a terrible torture for the leather thongs were weighted with bits of metal or wood. Jesus must have been considerably weakened by this ordeal. A Roman citizen had the right to die by the sword, but slaves and criminals were put to death by crucifixion. Apparently Jesus was unable to carry the cross-bar to the place of execution (in this case outside the city walls) as was customary. So a man called Simon of Cyrene was press-ganged into helping him. Mark names his sons, presumably already known to his readers, so Simon himself must have become a disciple.

Jesus was crucified between two robbers at a place called Golgotha (Latin: Calvary) at nine in the morning *(15: 22–47)*. He was fastened naked to the cross, so his clothes were divided by lot amongst the duty soldiers. The inscription showing the charge against him read 'King of the Jews'. When he was offered drugged wine, a gift from some charitable women in Jerusalem, he refused. After his flogging, he had been subjected to mockery by the soldiers. Again here, the passers-by, the chief priests and the scribes jeered at him. 'He saved others, but he cannot save himself,' they said. 'Let the Messiah, the King of Israel, come down from the cross. If we see that, we shall believe.' There was bitter truth in the gibe about saving himself. Jesus' whole ministry was spent in an endeavour to help others to a knowledge of God and their own deepest needs so that they were free to seek for the kingdom and realise it within themselves. He could have saved himself if he had taken another course.

Mark says that darkness fell upon the land between noon and three in the afternoon. While this may have been caused by a sandstorm, it symbolises desolation of spirit. At three, Jesus cried aloud 'My God, my God, why hast thou forsaken me?' Mark gives the actual Aramaic phrase, these being the only words from the cross that he records. The agony in that cry is beyond our thought, but we know that intense suffering of body and mind can bring with it utter desolation. That such was Jesus' experience only confirms his complete humanity. It also must be remembered, however, that *Psalm 22* opens with these precise words. The anguish of the psalmist was very apparent, yet somehow through his ordeal, he found his faith again and knew that God had not deserted him. The last words of the psalm are 'The Lord has acted'. We have already seen how Jesus frequently used phrases from the scriptures as a kind of shorthand to illustrate and clarify his situation. It is therefore possible that in his agony and sense of isolation from God, he turned to the psalm. With his dying, limited strength he was only able to say aloud the first line of the passage he knew so well. In his spirit he may well have completed it.

The bystanders thought Jesus was crying for Elijah. One of them ran with a sponge soaked in sour wine and held it to Jesus' lips. The resulting sharp intake of breath may well have been responsible for Jesus' actual death for he gave a loud cry and expired. As the body was stretched taut on the cross, the lungs would have been fully extended and therefore unable to expand further. Mysteriously at that moment the curtain of the innermost shrine of the Temple was torn in two. Seeing the manner in which Jesus had met his death, the centurion on duty at the crucifixion paid an extraordinary tribute to his prisoner, 'This man must have been a son of God'.

The faithful group of women who had been with Jesus and his disciples and had supported them all through his ministry, were present at this dreadful scene, even if they could not get very near. Mark names Mary Magdalene and Mary, the mother of James the younger and Joses, but not Jesus' mother, although in John's gospel she is present at the foot of the cross. Joseph of Arimathaea, a respected member of the Sanhedrin, who 'looked forward to the Kingdom of God, bravely went in to Pilate and asked for the body of Jesus'. He was probably a disciple of Jesus in private for it required great devotion to approach Pilate in this way. Pilate was surprised that Jesus had died in six hours when crucifixion victims could linger as long as a day or two. When he had made sure from the centurion that Jesus was dead, he gave Joseph permission to take the body. The arrangements had to be made quickly for the Sabbath would begin at six that evening. A further complication was that a criminal's death rendered a man religiously 'unclean' so he could not be buried within his family's grave. Joseph, however, wrapped Jesus in a linen sheet and laid him in a rock tomb, rolling a stone to block the entrance. Mary Magdalene and the other Mary saw where Jesus had been entombed. They planned to come after the Sabbath with aromatic oils for the anointing of the body.

Having bought these oils when the Sabbath was ended, the two Marys and Salome (16:1–8), got up 'just after sunrise' on the first day of the week and went to the tomb, only realising on their way there that they needed help in moving the very large stone. However, they found it had already been rolled back. 'They went into the tomb, where they saw a young man sitting on the right hand side, wearing a white robe; and they were dumbfounded.' The young man told them not to be afraid for Jesus had risen. They must return to the disciples, especially Peter, and tell them that Jesus would meet them all again in Galilee. This confirms the assurance that Jesus had given his friends on the way to Gethsemane *(14:28)*. Awestruck, the women fled from the tomb. They were too afraid to speak.

Scholarly opinion agrees that the gospel of Mark ends here. The second part of verse 8 and verses 9–20 are regarded as Epilogues for the two oldest Greek manuscripts omit these verses. Not only is their style different from the rest of the gospel, but the content of these verses is merely a summary of material dealt with more fully in *Luke, Acts* and *John*. Various explanations have been put forward for the gospel's abrupt ending, which must have been considered so unsatisfactory that additions were regarded as essential. Mark may have been interrupted, perhaps even arrested, as some believe that his last sentence is incomplete, hence the rather clumsy addition to verse 8. Maybe the end of the papyrus scroll was torn and lost. We can be sure that neither Matthew or Luke knew of any further ending to *Mark*, because they would have used it if they had. Their resurrection narratives differ from each other which means they used their own sources. Perhaps Mark meant to end his gospel where he did but if so Jesus' own promise, 'Nevertheless, after I am raised I shall go ahead of you into Galilee' *(14:28)* is unfulfilled as well as the words heard by the women at the empty tomb. Many scholars regard *John 21* as an appendix to that gospel. It could be, therefore, that John's account of the risen Jesus in Galilee was essentially Mark's lost ending, especially as in it Peter is reinstated by his Master after his thrice denial. Three times the Master asks Peter if he loves him, and after each reply, Peter is commissioned by Jesus to tend and feed his sheep.

I see no reason to quarrel with the early tradition that Peter was the inspiration behind Mark's gospel. In it we are given a vivid picture of Jesus, the complete human being and also the disciples' inability to grasp his significance until much later. The gospel contains the specific promise of the resurrection which is confirmed by the gospel titles of Jesus as the Christ, the Son of God, even though these are very sparingly used. There is also a continuity within the gospel with the picture of Peter in *Acts*, and with the message contained in the *1 Peter* epistle.
In the first half of *Acts*, Peter's leading role in the young community is clearly demonstrated. He preaches four sermons which give a clear picture of how the early disciples gave witness to their faith. There are also four passages in which Jesus is called the servant of God *(3:13; 3:26; 4:27; 4:30)* which may have been Peter's own title for Jesus. The universalism latent in the gospel is expressed by Peter's missionary work, especially his

conversion of the Roman centurion, Cornelius, which met with some opposition *(Acts 11:2,3)*. Peter disappears from the scene after his escape from prison *(Acts 12:17)* but by then James, the brother of Jesus is already head of the Jerusalem church. We hear indirectly of Peter from Paul's letters including a reference to the risen Jesus' appearance to him on the third day *(1 Corinthians 15:5)*. It may be that Peter was close to Paul. He certainly supported him at the Council of Jerusalem *(Acts 15:6–11)*. They knew Mark and each other very well.

TJ

PART TWO

Other New Testament witnesses to Jesus

Introduction

In our study of Mark, we have been aware of several notable omissions from his presentation of Jesus. For example we have no infancy or resurrection narratives, no Sermon on the Mount which includes the Lord's Prayer and comparatively few Parables compared with the other two synoptic gospels. In the study of Luke's and Matthew's gospels, I intend to concentrate on their distinctive contribution to the New Testament witness to Jesus. I hope that those readers to whom perhaps either *Luke* or *Matthew* is a favourite, will not feel that I have done these two gospels less than justice!

CHAPTER EIGHT

Luke

Authorship

Evidence from the second century leads us to regard Luke as the author of both the third gospel and the acts of the Apostles. The earliest writer who definitely named Luke as the author of these two books was Irenaeus, Bishop of Lyons ca. AD 185. The second piece of evidence is contained in a second-century manuscript fragment ca. AD 190, giving a list of scriptures acknowledged by the church in Rome [named after its first editor L. A. Muratori].

'The third book of the Gospel, that according to Luke, was compiled in his own name on Paul's authority by Luke the physician, when after Christ's ascension Paul had taken him to be with him like a legal expert. Yet neither did **he** see the Lord in the flesh; and he too, as he was able to ascertain events, begins his story from the birth of John.'

This important link with Paul is substantiated by Paul's letters where Luke is mentioned three times:

Colossians 4:14, 'Greetings to you from our dear friend Luke, the doctor'.
Philemon 24, 'my fellow workers, Mark, Aristarchus, Demas and Luke'.
2 Timothy 4:10,11, 'apart from Luke I have no one with me'.

In the *Acts of the Apostles*, the first person 'we' is rather unexpectedly introduced into the text: *(Acts 16:10–17; 20:5-15; 21:1–18; 27:1 – 28:16)*. This could mean that Luke kept a travel diary. In all probability he first joined Paul at Troas in Asia Minor (ca. AD 50) and went with him on the second missionary journey. He accompanied Paul from Philippi to Troas and was with him on his final journey up to Jerusalem (ca. AD 57). Later he and Paul stayed with Philip the Evangelist (one of the original seven deacons) at Caesarea and with Mnason 'a Christian from the early days' before they eventually arrived at Jerusalem. He must have been with Paul throughout the difficult days in Jersalem, Paul's arrest and two year imprisonment in Caesarea (ca. AD 57–59) when he would have had ample opportunity to collect material for his gospel from others like Mnason who were first generation Christians. Lastly, according to *Acts 27:1 – 28:16* he accompanied Paul on his hazardous journey to Rome and was with him during his two full years of imprisonment (ca. AD 60–62).

With regard to date and place of writing, there are two parameters: we can assume both that Luke wrote his gospel after Mark, as he uses Mark, and that the third gospel was sufficiently well known to be mentioned by Clement of Rome in AD 96. Many scholars, therefore, date the gospel between AD 75–85, although it has also been attributed to the AD 60s or even earlier by John T. Robinson. Later dating is fashionable with those who seek to question the validity of the record, while early dating poses challenging problems of interpetation. To my thinking, the length of time between the event and the written record does not fundamentally change the validity of the first experience; it changes the perspective from which it is viewed.

The place of writing is simply not known. In a second century prefatory note to the gospel Luke was described as a Syrian from Antioch, a doctor by profession, an associate of Paul until Paul's martyrdom, and dying at the age of 84 in central Greece; so both Syrian Antioch and Corinth have been suggested as possibilities!

Purpose in writing

In his preface, Luke clearly states why he has undertaken to write his gospel. 'To Theophilus: Many writers have undertaken to draw up an account of the events that have taken place among us, following the traditions handed down to us by the original eyewitnesses and servants of the gospel. So I in my turn, as one who has investigated the whole course of these events in detail, have decided to write an orderly narrative for you, your excellency, so as to give you authentic knowledge about the matters of which you have been informed.'

Several things emerge here. First this introduction is written in very good, stylish Greek and it follows the literary tradition of that time. Second, Luke addresses Theophilus (literally 'Friend of God') with the title 'your excellency'. It would be fair to assume therefore, that he was a high ranking educated Roman official, for in *Acts*, Luke uses the same title for a Roman governor *(Acts 23:26)*. It is possible that 'Theophilus' itself was a pseudonym or even a baptismal name but the fact that Luke wants to give him authentic knowledge of the Jesus story, suggests that this man had not yet taken the step of completely committing himself to baptism. Third, Luke says of himself that he has not been an eyewitness to these events but he claims that he has undertaken a thorough investigation into all the facts and has had the chance to assess the record, so that Theophilus may have **accurate** and true knowledge about the faith in Jesus the Christ.

Luke must also have had in mind that his readers would not only be this particular man but many others of a similar type, whom Theophilus represented – in other words educated Gentiles. Hence when studying the striking characteristics of his gospel, we shall see that for Luke, Jesus the Christ is much more than the Jewish Messiah; he is the **Saviour of the World**. His favourite title for Jesus is **Lord**, which he uses at least 12 times. As he also dedicated *Acts* to Theophilus, he obviously intended his two volume work to be read as one book. In it he is clearly recommending Christianity as the religion for the Roman Empire. In this sense his writing is the first Christian apologia.

Content

Luke uses Mark's gospel, which he handles with respect, apart from correcting Mark's grammar and style. However he discards 35% of this gospel, omitting for example, the small details which in *Mark* seem to indicate an eye witness account, the touches which give us Jesus' emotions and which show the disciples' failure to understand Jesus.

Mark 10:14 – 'They (the mothers) brought children for him to touch. The disciples rebuked them, but when Jesus saw it he was indignant'.
Luke 18:15,16 – 'They brought babies for him to touch, and when the disciples saw them, they rebuked them. But Jesus called for the children'.
Mark 4:39,40 – 'The wind dropped and there was dead calm. He said to them, "Why are you such cowards? Have you no faith even now?"'.
Luke 8:24,25 – 'The storm subsided and there was calm. "Where is your faith?" he asked'.

Luke omits Jesus' words to his three friends in the garden of Gethsemane, 'My heart is ready to break with grief' *(Mark 14:33,34)*, but he does not minimise Jesus' suffering 'and in anguish of spirit he prayed the more urgently; and his sweat was like drops of blood falling to the ground' *(Luke 22:44)*.
Luke also omits Jesus' cry of desolation from the cross *(Mark 15:34)* but gives instead three other words full of forgiveness, consolation and finally a sense of completion, 'Father, into your hands, I commit my spirit' *(Luke 23:34,43,46)*.

The Jesus of Luke's gospel is **not** devoid of feeling or humanity. He is full of tender compassion and we shall note many examples in detail. One will suffice to make the point here. Luke records that Jesus actually wept over the tragic fate of Jerusalem *(13:34–5; 19:41–4)*. Luke has a different perspective from Mark and his interpretation of Jesus is influenced by his whole approach. It fully endorses Mark's witness but adds another dimension which we must recognise and appreciate.

Besides *Mark*, Luke uses two further sources and it is these which comprise the bulk of his gospel.
First, both he and Matthew share a common source, i.e. material which consists mostly of the Sayings of Jesus. This provides his shortened version of the Sermon on the Mount *(6:22–49)* and his record of the Lord's Prayer *(11:1–4)*.
Second, there is material which is not found elselwhere, which must derive from Luke's own individual research and knowledge. This consists of –
The birth stories of John Baptist and Jesus, *chapters 1 and 2*.
A great deal of *chapters 7:1 – 8:3* and the long section 9:51 – 19:44.
Certain sections of the Passion narrative *chapters 22–23*.
The Resurrection narrative, *chapter 24*.

It is more than probable that Luke collected this material, either in oral or written form, when he was staying in the region during Paul's two year imprisonment. He would have access to the accounts of first generation Christians. From the evidence in the first two chapters, it has even been suggested that Luke may have met Mary, the mother of Jesus, or people who had been close to her:

'But Mary treasured up all these things and pondered over them' *(2:19)*.

'The child's father and mother were full of wonder at what was being said about him. Simeon blessed them and said to Mary his mother, "This child is destined to be a sign that will be rejected and you too will be pierced to the heart"' *(2:33–34)*.

'His parents were astonished to see him there, and his mother said to him "My son, why have you treated us like this? Your father and I have been anxiously searching for you". "Why did you search for me?" he said. "Did you not know that I was bound to be in my Father's House?" But they did not understand what he meant. Then he went back with them to Nazareth, and continued to be under their authority; his mother treasured up all these things in her heart' *(2:49–51)*.

CHAPTER NINE

Luke's special contribution

1. We owe it to Luke, that we can place **Jesus squarely in history**, for he gives us certain dates according to Roman emperors and Jewish officials. He begins his gospel with the events leading up to the birth of John, son of the priest, Zechariah. John was to be the herald of the Messiah and he baptised people in preparation for his momentous coming. Herod the Great's dates are 37–4 BC. 'In the reign of Herod king of Judaea, there was a priest named Zechariah' *(1:5)*. He then proceeds to explain why it was that Joseph and Mary went from their home in Nazareth to Bethlehem in Judea. 'In those days a decree was issued by the emperor Augustus for a census to be taken throughout the Roman world. This was the first registration of its kind; it took place when Quirinius was governor of Syria. Everyone made his way to his own home town. Joseph went up to Judaea from the town of Nazareth in Galilee, to register in the city of David, called Bethlehem, because he was of the house of David by descent; and with him went Mary, his betrothed, who was expecting her child. While they were there the time came for her to have her baby, and she gave birth to a son, her firstborn' *(2:1–7)*.

Augustus Caesar, the first emperor (31 BC – AD 14), initiated enrolments as a useful means of obtaining administrative information to govern the empire. According to Egyptian sources, these took place every 14 years, by households. Quirinius could have been twice governor of Syria (of which Judaea was a part) and there is some evidence to suggest that he held a census during each term of office. Josephus, the Jewish historian, speaks of the Quirinius census held in AD 6, which provoked a serious uprising of the Zealots under Judas of Galilee. This, however, is an impossibly late date for Jesus' birth as Herod died in 4 BC. There could have been an earlier census, held with Herod's agreement, during Quirinius' first governship. On the other hand, Josephus implies that 'all the people of the Jews' were required to make an oath of allegiance to Augustus and Herod about this time, so Luke may have confused the census of loyalty with the later enrolment. In any case there is no external evidence (as yet!) to confirm Luke's statement that the census in which Joseph was involved was 'the first census of the whole Roman world'. Whatever census took place, it probably only concerned the Jewish world.

In the 4th century, Constantine the Great made Christianity the official religion of the Empire. Subsequently, using all the information then available, attempts were made in the 6th century to find out the exact date of Jesus' birth, hence the division of history into BC, and AD. Although scholars today have a more accurate means of calculating these dates, and consequently place Jesus' birth somewhere around 6 BC, it would be futile now to change western historical dating.

Luke also gives a further date for the preaching of John Baptist. 'In the 15th year of the emperor Tiberius, when Pontius Pilate was governor of Judaea, when Herod was tetrarch of Galilee, his brother Philip, prince of Iturea and Trachonitis and Lysanias prince of Abilene; during the high-priesthood of Annas and Caiaphas, the word of God came to John, son of Zechariah in the wilderness' *(3:1–2)*. It is not necessary to go into detail about these dates as attention can be focussed on Tiberius, who became joint emperor with Augustus in AD 11–12, so the 15th year of his reign would be AD 26–7. Tiberius became sole successor in AD 14, so if Luke meant 15 years from then, the date would be AD 29. Pontius Pilate's dates as Procurator of Judaea, were AD 26–30. Annas was succeeded by his son-in-law Caiaphas as High Priest, but retained the courtesy title.

At one time the veracity of Luke's historical data was much questioned, but more recent archaeological research has confirmed rather than diminished his accuracy.

2. Luke presents **Jesus as a figure of universal importance** whose mission is to the whole of humanity rather than simply to the Jewish nation. He also strongly emphasises Jesus' own grief at his rejection by his own people and what he sees to be the tragic consequences for the Jews of this attitude.

(a) The conception of Jesus: Luke recounts not only the unusual circumstances of John Baptist's conception, but also the angelic visitation to Mary, the betrothed of Joseph *(1:26–36)*. According to the literal interpretation of this event, Mary conceived Jesus through the action of the Holy Spirit rather than Joseph. However when he compiled Jesus' family tree (which is found also with variations in Matthew's gospel), Luke traces Jesus back through Joseph not Mary, who may have been of Levitical descent. The point of this genealogical exercise is to prove that Jesus was the Son of David, heir of the royal house, and as descendant of Abraham,

55

inheritor of God's promise *(Genesis 22:18; 12:1–3)*, which is where Matthew's account finishes. Luke, however, takes Jesus right back to Adam, whom he would believe to be an actual historical person, to show that Jesus had significance for the whole human race.

According to Matthew, Joseph 'took Mary home to be his wife' *(1:25)*. Presumably Mary's child was then legally recognised as Joseph's son, but for the genealogy to be meaningful, his male ancestry must be by blood not adoption.

Looking at the Annunciation *(1:26–38)* in the context of Luke's imagery throughout his gospel, I am not convinced that Luke intended his readers to think that a virgin conception took place. Mary's betrothal to Joseph was as binding as marriage, for if a betrothed virgin had sexual intercourse with a man who was not her betrothed, she could be convicted of adultery. Mary, in her vision, was told by Gabriel (in Old Testament belief, one of the four archangels) that she was to be the mother of the Messiah. She was as yet a virgin, but 'The Holy Spirit will come upon you, and the power of the Most High will overshadow you; for that reason the holy child to be born will be called Son of God' *(1:35)*. The language used is an echo of the Genesis account of creation: 'The earth was a vast waste, darkness covered the deep, and the spirit of God hovered over the surface of the water' *(1:2)*. As God's spirit was active at the beginning of all things, so now the Spirit would endow this child with quite exceptional qualities. He was to be the beginning of a new chapter in human history.

At that time, and for several subsequent centuries, the male seed was thought to contain the perfectly formed human being, the woman's womb being only the bed in which it was placed. (Hence the disgrace to the woman if she proved barren.) It is difficult to reconcile this belief with the idea of a virgin conception where no male seed is planted in the womb. Although the Jews used a masculine pronoun for God, their concept had no sexual connotations whatsoever. In any case why was a virgin conception necessary? The Old Testament had a very healthy view of sexual relationships and regarded conception and the birth of a child as a gift from God. Sometimes through the blessing of God, conception took place when all hope had gone as in the case of Zechariah and Elizabeth whose story preceded that of Mary. John also was a special child endowed with great gifts.

But the most important argument against virgin conception is not a question of physical grounds at all. To present Jesus as less than fully human seriously detracts from his message and his life. He had to come to terms, in his own human nature, with the complexities that we all experience. The Genesis myth of the so called 'Fall' *(ch.3)*, is, I believe, a brilliant attempt to explain in parabolic form the contradictory impulses that face us: we can dream of a perfect world and yet experience something quite other. The subsequent doctrine of 'original sin' ceased to be valid when it was recognised that Adam was a pictorial representation, not in any way a real person. Our potential for good and evil, for creative love and self-destructive egotism has to be resolved here and now if we are to progress at all as a species. For me, it is therefore essential, that we see Jesus as the product of Mary and Joseph's love, whatever Matthew's gospel may say to the contrary.

(b) Luke gives us other examples of the universal nature of Jesus' mission. At the very beginning of his ministry he shows Jesus being rejected by his own people in Nazareth *(4:16–30)*. According to his account, Jesus attended a synagogue service in his home town, read the lesson appointed for that day which included *Isaiah 61:1–2*:

> The spirit of the Lord is upon me because he has anointed me;
> he has sent me to announce good news to the poor,
> to proclaim release for prisoners and recovery of sight for the blind;
> to let the broken victims go free, to proclaim the year of the Lord's favour.

Jesus then astonished the congregation by saying 'Today, in your hearing this text has come true'. They reacted with admiration and doubt 'Is this not Joseph's son?' they asked. Jesus then referred back to two great Old Testament prophets, Elijah *(1 Kings 17–18)* and Elisha *(2 Kings 5)* who worked miracles of healing for the Sidonian widow at Sarepta and for the Syrian leper, Naaman. By implication, his own mission would be to the Gentiles, if his fellow countrymen were to ignore him. They did so. The congregation reacted in fury and thrust Jesus out of the town.

(c) The healing of the Centurion's servant *(7:1–10)* is a remarkable story which is worth comparing with the healing of the Syro-Phoenician woman's daughter in *Mark (7:24–30)*. In both cases a Gentile child is healed unseen, through the faith of mother or master. In Luke's account, the Centurion was well aware of Jewish sensibilities regarding contact with non-Jews. He approached Jesus, therefore, first through Jewish elders in Capernaum for whom he had built a synagogue, second through his friends who relayed his actual words. 'Do not trouble further, sir; I am not worthy to have you come under my roof, and that is why I did not approach you in person. But say the word and my servant will be cured. I know, for I am myself under orders, with soldiers under me.' He recognised in Jesus a great spiritual authority. The climax comes in Jesus' comparison 'I tell you, not even in Israel, have I found such faith'.

(d) In the parable of the Good Samaritan *(10:25–37)*, it was the despised half-caste, ritually outside Judaism, who had the inner perception to understand who was his neighbour. He needed no legalistic definition but responded with compassion to someone in dire need. This was in sharp contrast to the attitudes of the priest and the Levite whose main concern was for the niceties of ritual requirements, i.e. to avoid any ceremonially unclean contact with blood and death.

(e) When he told the parable of the Great Feast *(14:15–24)*, Jesus was being entertained by a leading Pharisee whose motives were not of the most generous: 'they were watching him closely'. In response to some pious platitudes about the happiness of 'those who will sit at the feast in the kingdom of God!', Jesus tells his own allegory. The host was God; the banquet, the supreme blessing of the kingdom; the servant was Jesus; the double invitation to the guests, who were the righteous Jews, was in accordance with Jerusalem custom. Each of the guests made some excuse for non-attendance at the feast. The host was furious and sent out his servant on two further missions. First, to gather in the poor and other disadvantaged people, who represented the irreligious Jews because, in the story, they were all within the city walls. Second, the servant went outside the city and gathered in others to come to the feast. These represented the Gentiles. Although we might find it offensive that others 'outside the wall' were included only as a last resort we have to see the point of the whole story and its relation to Jesus' cultural setting. The striking thing is that he should even consider God's kingdom to be available for all people not the chosen few. He also states that those who reject it do so by their own choice. Their completely wrong perspective causes Jesus much anguish.

(f) Having been asked to cure 10 lepers *(17:11–19)*, Jesus told the men to go and show themselves to the priest. This was necessary so that they could be certified clean and could offer suitable sacrifices to God. They would then be allowed to enter fully into the community again. In an act of faith, the men obeyed Jesus and were on their way to the priest when the miracle happened and they were cured. Only one of the men, a Samaritan, came back to thank Jesus. Jesus wryly commented – 'Were not all 10 made clean? . . . Was no one found returning to give praise to God except this foreigner?' Then he gave the man the further gift of wholeness.

(g) Luke's resurrection narrative tells us that Jesus' disciples were charged to take their message of the forgiveness of sins 'to **all nations** beginning from Jerusalem' *(24:27)*.

(h) In small details, Luke is aware of his Gentile readership. His use of the title Lord, for Jesus, has Gentile significance; his substitution of teacher for rabbi, and lawyer for scribe, makes his approach clear.

3. Luke himself must have had **strong social sympathies** for he certainly is aware of Jesus' own concern for those who were poor, outcast and, in the case of women, the humbler members of society. Part of his special section, i.e. *chs. 15:1 – 19:44* has been called the Gospel of the Outcast. Some outstanding examples of this special characteristic of the third gospel are given below:

(a) Various incidents concern **women**:

(i) The healing of the widow's son at Nain *(7:11–17)* is represented as a miraculous raising from the dead, but we have to take into consideration a comparable Old Testament story in which Elijah *(1 Kings 17:17–24)* restored to life the son of a Shunamite woman especially as Shunam was only two miles from Nain. The point for us is that Jesus felt intense compassion for the widow whose only support had been taken away from her by her son's illness. Jesus entered the city as the funeral was leaving it. He touched the bier containing the corpse thereby making himself ceremonially unclean for at least seven days. Then he spoke 'Young man, I tell you to get up,' which he did. My own interpretation would be that the widow's son was in a deep coma, presumed dead, but the healing was nevertheless an awesome feat.

(ii) Jesus and the Prostitute *(7:36–50)*. We are not told the name of the city where Jesus had been preaching but obviously both Simon the Pharisee and the woman 'who was living an immoral life' had heard him. Simon was frankly curious about Jesus, had invited him to supper but was neglectful of two of the usual acts of courtesy, i.e. offering Jesus water to wash his feet and giving him the respectful kiss of peace. No doubt the house was open and guests would recline on couches with their feet away from the table. Thus it was possible for the woman to approach Jesus so as to wash his feet with her tears, wipe them with her hair, kiss them and anoint them with myrrh. This most extravagant gesture of love was quietly accepted by Jesus, much to the horror of Simon for whom the woman would have been quite untouchable. Jesus discerned not only Simon's criticism of him but also that the woman's outpouring of love was the result of a profound inner change in response to Jesus' teaching. The lesson of his parable is simply that the one who has been forgiven most, loves most. He then publicly reinstated the woman by saying 'Your sins are forgiven'. A miracle of transformation had taken place. And Jesus further endorsed it by adding 'Your faith has saved you; go in peace'.

(iii) It is helpful to link the Martha and Mary *(10:38–42)* incident to what John's gospel *(ch. 11)* tells us about the sisters. They lived in

59

Bethany (a village not far from Jerusalem), with their brother, Lazarus. Martha was obviously the head of the household. Luke's chronology must be wrong here, as in *chapter 10* Jesus was still a long way from Jerusalem. but most probably the passage fitted best into this context where Luke's theme is discipleship. Martha was preoccupied with the dutiful care of her guest and was irritated that her sister, instead of coming to help her, stayed listening to Jesus. His loving comment to Martha is significant for two reasons: first, women have as much right as men to be his disciples and receive his teaching; second, although the practicalities of life are necessary and important, a sense of perspective is always needed. If we intuitively apprehend priorities, we can respond to a particular situation with undivided attention. I believe Martha got the point, for in John's gospel she makes a supreme declaration of faith. When Jesus asks if she believes he is the resurrection and the life, she answers: 'I do, Lord. I believe that you are the Messiah, the Son of God who has come into the world'.

(iv) Jesus performs a Sabbath Day healing for a poor crippled woman *(13:10–17)*, who had suffered for 18 years from some kind of curvature of the spine. According to scribal writ, Sabbath healing was only permitted if life was in danger, but Jesus, out of compassion, called her to him and said 'You are rid of your trouble'. When he laid his hands on her, she was able to straighten up. The President of the Synagogue criticised Jesus for being a Sabbath-breaker. Jesus could not stand such hypocrisy. If a man was permitted to care for his cattle on the Sabbath, why could not this woman be 'loosed from her bonds on the Sabbath?'

(v) It is from *Luke (8:2,3)* that we learn of the band of women (including Mary of Magdala and Joanna, wife of Chuza, a steward of Herod) who accompanied Jesus and the Twelve disciples on their journeys and who 'provided for them out of their own resources'. These women were in, every way, disciples of Jesus.

(vi) Two of Jesus' parables touch on the life of women: one has to do with a woman baking bread *(13:20)*: 'To what shall I compare the kingdom of God? It is like yeast which a woman took and mixed with three measures of flour till it was all leavened'. The other was in answer to the basic criticism levelled against Jesus by the Pharisees and scribes that 'This fellow (Jesus), welcomes sinners and eats with them' *(15:1–10)*. The reply of Jesus consisted in several examples of God's love, amongst them – 'If a woman has 10 silver coins and loses one of them, does she not light the lamp, sweep out the house, and look in every corner till she finds it? And when she does, she calls her friends and neighbours together and says "Rejoice with me! I have found the coin that I lost". In the same way, I tell you, there is joy among the angels of God over one sinner who repents'.

(b) Concern for **the sinner and the outcast**: The Pharisees held that the way of holiness meant separation from all possible contamination. Jesus was therefore irreligious because he was always in contact with the most undesirable members of the community. He dealt with this criticism in two ways.

First: He defined what he considered to be God's attitude to those who had strayed from the right path. The parables of the Lost Sheep, the Lost Coin and the Prodigal Son (15:11–32) are probably the clearest exposition of this teaching. A further point is made in the latter parable, for the father (who represents God) not only shows his abiding love for his younger son, who had grievously sinned, but also for his righteous elder son, 'you are always with me and everything I have is yours'. The constant love of the father eventually drew the younger son home, in changed frame of heart and mind and his father's joyous welcome enabled him to begin life anew. The elder brother resented this generosity, for he had by now quite rejected his brother. He spoke of him as 'this son of yours'. But the father reaffirmed the kinship 'How could we fail to celebrate this happy day? Your brother here was dead and has come back to life; he was lost and has been found'.

Second: He strongly condemned both Pharisees and scribes for their spiritual blindness, pride and hypocrisy (11:37–54). For Jesus, religious purity sprang entirely from right motivation (cf. Mark 7:1–23). But with the Pharisees the outward proprieties were all important – 'You Pharisees clean the outside of cup and plate, but inside you are full of greed and wickedness'. They were obsessed with the trivialities of law keeping. 'Alas for you Pharisees! You pay tithes of mint and rue and every garden herb, but neglect justice and the love of God. It is these you should have practised without overlooking the others. Alas for you Pharisees! You love to have the chief seats in the synagogue and to be greeted respectfully in the street.' He was angry that the lawyers in their interpretation and practice of the letter of the law, 'load men with intolerable burdens, and will not lift a finger to lighten the load'. The only prophets they honoured were dead ones who would cause no trouble. 'Alas for you lawyers! You have taken away the key of knowledge. You did not go in yourselves, and those who were trying to go in, you prevented.' Obviously Jesus was referring to knowledge of the one true living God which was the key to the kingdom or reign of love.

A parable and an incident illustrate these points:

In the story (18:9–14) a certain Pharisee went into the temple to pray. His prayer consisted of a catalogue of his own virtues. 'I thank you, God, that I am not like the rest of mankind.' A second man was also in the temple, praying. He was a tax collector and very aware of his own condition 'God, have mercy on me, sinner that I am'. Because the tax-collector had the self-knowledge to ask God to meet his need, he received forgiveness and renewal. The Pharisee was not open to receive anything. Jesus' warning on self-righteousness is clear. The Pharisees' tragedy was that though they lived exemplary lives themselves, they despised others for not maintaining the same high standards.

On his way up to Jerusalem, Jesus passed through Jericho, an important customs station. The superintendent of taxes there, Zacchaeus by name and a very rich man, was 'eager to see Jesus' *(19:1–10)*. Jesus spotted him perched in a sycamore tree and said 'Be quick and come down, for I must stay at your house today'. There was a 'general murmur of disapproval' for Zacchaeus was disliked and a 'sinner'. However, Zacchaeus' response to Jesus was very moving. 'Here and now, sir, I give half my possessions to charity; and if I have defrauded anyone I will repay him four times over.' Jesus reinstated him: he now belonged to the 'true' Israel, for 'The Son of Man has come to seek and to save what is lost'.

Jesus' intense love for 'lost' people endured to the end *(23:34,40–43)*. Given the agony of death by crucifixion, it is a quite extraordinary tribute to his compassion and unique understanding of human nature that he was able to say, 'Father, forgive them; they do not know what they are doing'. And when the criminal crucified at his side recognised Jesus' innocence and appealed to him to 'remember me when you come to your throne', Jesus summoned the strength and faith to respond; 'Truly I tell you, today you will be with me in Paradise'.

(c) The **condemnation of love of money and pride** is a corollary of Jesus' support for the under-privileged. One day *(12:16–21)*, Jesus was asked to adjudicate between two brothers who were wrangling about their inheritance. He refused; 'Who set me over you to judge or arbitrate?' To the crowd, he said 'Beware! Be on your guard against greed of every kind, for even when someone has more than enough, his possessions do not give him life'. Then he told the parable of the Rich Fool who selfishly amassed a large fortune so that he could 'take life easy, eat, drink and enjoy' himself, but he died that very night so of what good to him was his money then? 'That is how it is with the man who piles up treasure for himself and remains a pauper in the eyes of God.'

Jesus firmly believed that death was not the end and that how a person lived now would enable or disable them for the next life. The parable of the rich man and Lazarus *(16:19–31)* pointed to the futility of an entirely selfish life. The rich man in the story probably depicted a typical Sadducee who did not believe in a life after death. His sumptuous life style was contrasted with the bleak picture of Lazarus, covered with sores, lying in abject poverty at the entrance to the rich man's house. When Lazarus died, he was 'carried away by the angels to be with Abraham'. When the rich man died, he went to Hades, the underworld. There, in torment, he glimpsed far away, Abraham and Lazarus beside him. He made three requests; that Lazarus himself should be allowed (i) to alleviate his suffering; (ii) warn his five brothers of the dreadful fate awaiting them; and (iii) return from the dead to reinforce the message. Abraham replied 'If they do not listen to Moses and the prophets, they will pay no heed even if someone should rise from the dead'.

In this story, Jesus used the current Pharisaic belief of rewards and punishments after death to highlight the personal spiritual disaster of a completely selfish way of life. But within the concept of a God of Love, there can be no such condition as eternal torment. The reference to Moses and the prophets reminds us of Jesus' answer to the Sadducean question about life after death, as reported in *Mark (12:24–27)*. John's account of the raising of Lazarus *(ch. 11)* and the resurrection experiences of Jesus' first disciples clearly illustrate the truth of the parable's final sentence, 'If they do not listen to Moses and the prophets they will pay no heed even if someone should rise from the dead'.

CHAPTER TEN

The poetry in Luke's gospel

LUKE'S APPRECIATION AND USE OF POETIC IMAGERY is one of the things
which makes his gospel so attractive. He may even have been a poet himself.
At the beginning of his story he includes three poems. The songs of Mary, of
Zechariah, and of Simeon, have been used in Christian worship for
centuries. Mary's song, known as the Magnificat from the first word in
Latin, is reminiscent of Hannah's prayer of thanksgiving to God (*1 Samuel
2:1–10*). For many years Hannah, to her great grief, had remained
childless, then 'the Lord remembered her; she conceived, and in due time
bore a son'. The Magnificat (*1:46–55*) not only expresses Mary's personal
praise and gratitude, but also rejoices that the promise given to Abraham
will now be fulfilled. God's justice and mercy will be paramount – 'He has
routed the proud and all their schemes . . . raised on high the lowly. He has
filled the hungry with good things, and sent the rich away empty'.
Zechariah's hymn (*1:68–79*. Latin: Benedictus) is also full of praise to the
Lord, 'For he has turned to his people and set them free. He has raised for
us a strong deliverer from the house of his servant David'. It includes a
prophecy concerning his son, John, that he 'will be called Prophet of the
Most High . . . the Lord's forerunner, to prepare his way and lead his
people to a knowledge of salvation through the forgiveness of their sins'. It
ends with a beautiful image of the coming new age –

>For in the tender compassion of our God
>the dawn from heaven will break upon us,
>to shine on those who live in darkness, under the shadow of death,
>and to guide our feet into the way of peace.

Malachi 4:2 used similar words – 'for you, who fear my name, the sun of
righteousness will rise with healing in its wings' but the context is totally
different for Malachi was concerned with the forthcoming judgement of the
'great and terrible day of the Lord'.
Simeon's song (*2:29–32*. Latin: Nunc Dimittis) adds further insights into

the purpose of Jesus' mission. It will be not only to the Jews, but for the whole world: 'For I have seen with my own eyes the deliverance you have made ready in full view of all nations: a light that will bring revelation to the Gentiles and glory to your people Israel'.

The great themes in all three poems are an intrinsic part of Luke's gospel and form an introduction to what follows. For this reason, some scholars believe that Luke wrote the hymns himself. The authorship cannot be proved either way, for Mary (who could have been of Levitical descent: her cousin Elizabeth was married to a priest), Zechariah, and Simeon (probably a retired priest), would all have been capable of expressing these ideas resonant of Old Testament imagery from the psalms and prophets. Certainly the content of the poems would have come from Mary, Zechariah and Simeon, even if Luke rephrased it. However, the reader could well ask, if Luke did compose the poems and then attribute them to others, would this not make him dishonest and therefore an unreliable witness? I think the ancient mind did not place such importance on the kind of accuracy that we believe to be so significant. The question 'Is this true or not' meaning 'did it happen exactly like that' can be the wrong one to ask of any particular ancient document. The gap in time itself makes an answer to this question impossible. We cannot always rely on the accurate reporting of something that happened last week, because accounts of the occasion differ. We need to address ourselves to trying to understand what was the experiential truth or meaning of any particular event not only to the writer but also to his readers.
Luke was writing about the fundamental tenets of his faith and expressing them in imagery, poetry, symbol and familiar Old Testament language. He was communicating to a readership who shared his culture and his times as we do not. Instead we must make the necessary leap of imagination which can enable us to appreciate his vision even if we are not able to identify with it completely.

Luke's faithfulness, however, in reporting the words of Jesus cannot be in doubt. After all he believed that the truth of Jesus' teaching brought salvation to those who accepted it. Also, of course, Jesus' sayings were memorable because they were often couched in poetic parallelisms. For the first disciples, used to learning their scriptures by rote, the Master's life-giving teaching would be learnt without difficulty and passed on to others.

Five further instances will serve to illustrate the heightened vividness of Jesus' poetic phrasing and the power of his response to situations.
(i) Luke tells us how Jesus sent out 72 disciples (10:1–24). He has already recorded the mission of the Twelve (9:1–6). This account of a second missionary charge must have occurred in Luke's source and been included

65

by him in good faith. That Jesus did sent out his disciples on two separate occasions is not impossible, even if somewhat unlikely. The number 70 or 72 in Jewish number symbolism stood for the nations of the world. So as the mission of the Twelve was for the Jews, this second charge stood for the universal mission of Jesus' disciples to the world. The disciples returned 'jubilant'. They had experienced the power of the name of Jesus, the Lord, in casting out evil spirits. Jesus shared with them his own insight into their success, 'I saw Satan fall, like lightning from heaven'. He assured them that his power would continue for it was a sign of the presence of the kingdom, of love itself. He then prayed out loud to his Father; he did not use the Jewish way of speaking of God but always particularly addressed him as 'Abba' Father. (Burney described this prayer as a rhythmic poem.) His experiences of the Father have led him to believe that he knows God in a unique sense and is known by him. The knowledge of God and his purpose is not a matter of learning or cleverness, but of spiritual perception. Jesus is conscious of being chosen by the Father as means of revealing his truth to others: that truth comes as a result of relationship. His disciples are blessed for they are seeing the present reality of the kingdom. Past generations could only long and hope for its coming.

(ii) As we have seen from Mark's gospel, Jesus' opponents could not deny Jesus' power but they attributed it to Satan. In *Luke (11 : 14–23)* Jesus used the same argument to prove that his power could not be Satanic. He forcibly asserted, 'If it is by the finger of God that I drive out demons, then be sure that the kingdom of God has already come upon you'. (The 'finger of God' refers back to *Exodus 8 : 17–19*, when the Egyptian magicians gave up their unequal contest with Moses and Aaron.) He went on to make an absolute statement 'He who is not with me is against me, and he who does not gather with me scatters'. The image strikes a chord in the imagination. Although the sentence has been much misused by dictatorial regimes and in unscrupulous witchhunts where issues are always presented in black and white terms, there is a sense in which Jesus spoke profound truth. There are some issues about which there can be no neutrality or even compromise. To betray the cause of love and compassion is to deny the roots of humanity itself. The appalling treatment of the Jews and other minority groups in Hitler's concentration camps must be completely condemned as must the death of millions of dissenters in the Stalin era in Russia. It is the genius of Jesus that he draws a clear line between those who follow the dictates of love and truth and those who deliberately ignore them and walk the other way. In the course of our lives we inevitably need to make intelligent compromises on occasions and we are none of us compassionate and honest all the time. But if the naked intent of our will is directed towards the good, then we are walking the way of Jesus, however often we fail, and whether we know it or not.

(iii) In *Luke 12:35–39* Jesus discusses the future with his disciples. The time of crisis has now come upon them: they must be watchful. He speaks of his own conflict, pain and tension. (The REB version cannot do justice to the poetical form, but I have set it out in the appropriate lines.)

> I have come to set fire to the earth,
> and how I wish it were already kindled!
> I have a baptism to undergo,
> and what constraint I am under until it is over!
> Do you suppose I came to establish peace on earth?
> No indeed I have come to bring dissension.

And the section finishes with a picture of the divided family.

These words may come as a shock to those who think of Jesus as primarily the peace-maker. His love and compassion were such that to bring conflict into people's lives caused him great anguish. But we know that people in the prophetic mould are sometimes called to speak truth to power however great the disturbance they create. In our own times Martin Luther King, Gandhi, Desmond Tutu and Solzhenitsyn have disturbed and shaken people profoundly. In the Old Testament, the prophet Jeremiah felt the same terrible conflict.

> I am reproached and derided all the time
> for uttering the word of the Lord.
> Whenever I said, 'I shall not call it to mind
> or speak in his name again,'
> then his word became imprisoned within me
> like a fire burning in my heart.
> I was weary with holding it under,
> and could endure no more.   *Jeremiah 20:8,9*

(iv) As Jesus was struggling on his way to the place of crucifixion, 'great numbers of people followed, among them many women who mourned and lamented over him' *(23:27–31)*. He turned to them and said, 'Daughters of Jerusalem *(cf. Song of Songs 1:5)*, do not weep for me; weep for yourselves and your children. For the days are surely coming when people will say, "Happy are the barren, the womb that never bore a child, the breasts that never fed one"'. With his prophetic insight Jesus knew that a terrible time was coming for the people of that city: so terrible that childlessness would be a blessing rather than a deep humiliation, for at least mothers would not have the agony of seeing their children suffer. Then he added 'For if these things are done when the wood is green, what will happen when it is dry?'

67

(v) The last extract is not poetry in the strict sense of the word, but it is one of the most beautiful stories in *Luke* and sums up his beliefs *(24:1–35)*. After the death and burial of Jesus, the devoted women disciples went to the tomb on the first day of the week, and found it empty. Two men in dazzling garments spoke to them, 'Why search among the dead for one who is alive?' They returned to the men but their story was dismissed as nonsense. However, on the same day another disciple named Cleopas, with a companion, possibly his wife, was travelling from Jerusalem to Emmaus, when they were joined by a stranger, whom they did not recognise. During their walk together, they told the stranger of their great sorrow regarding Jesus and how their hopes in his messiahship had been shattered. 'How dull you are,' he answered, 'How slow to believe all that the prophets said.' Then he explained how inevitable it was that the Messiah should suffer and illuminated the scriptures for them. The two disciples asked the stranger to come in and stay overnight with them. During supper 'he broke the bread and offered it to them. Then their eyes were opened and they recognised him'. The resurrected Jesus vanished from their sight but they said to each other, 'Were not our hearts on fire when he talked with us on the road and explained the scriptures to us?' They returned to Jerusalem where Jesus appeared to the rest of his disciples.

Luke's second volume, *Acts*, is full of the joy of fellowship and the activity of the Holy Spirit, for the risen Jesus was experienced amongst his followers as the living Lord *(Acts 2:43–47)*. The story of two disciples walking together who felt the empowering and joyful presence of 'another' even 'the other', exemplified the faith of the young community and indeed has been the experience of many other people in succeeding centuries.

CHAPTER ELEVEN

Matthew

WHEN WE COME TO THIS GOSPEL, we are dealing with a somewhat different proposition from Mark and Luke. It is placed at the beginning of the New Testament because in previous centuries it was regarded as the work of Matthew the apostle, therefore authoritative. It has been used as the great teaching manual of the Christian church and would appear in some respects to have been written for this purpose.

Authorship

This first gospel reproduced some 90% of *Mark*, using his order and much of his language. But the vivid and realistic detail is missing and remarks, especially about the Twelve and Jesus' own human reactions to a situation are either toned down or omitted. Matthew leaves out altogether the conversation Jesus had with the disciples on the occasion of the healing of the woman with the haemorrhage and also the fact that Jesus took Peter, James and John with him to Jairus' house. When Jesus was rejected by most people at his home town of Nazareth, Matthew omits any comment about Jesus' own reaction to their lack of faith.

Mark 8:14–21, shows an exasperated Jesus saying to his friends 'Why are you talking about having no bread? Have you no inkling yet? Do you still not understand? Are your minds closed? You have eyes: can you not see? You have ears: can you not hear?' Although Matthew includes the words 'Why are you talking about having no bread? Where is your faith? Do you still not understand?' he adds another paragraph reinstating the disciples: 'Then they understood: they were to be on their guard, not against baker's leaven, but against the teaching of the Pharisees and Sadducees' *(16:12)*. Matthew fails to include Mark's comment that Jesus was very indignant with his disciples when they tried to prevent the mothers from bringing their children to Jesus to bless. Further, in the First gospel, it is the mother of James and John not the brothers themselves, who makes the request of Jesus, that her sons should have priority treatment.

Matthew also has a tendency to heighten the miraculous. Mark's moving and detailed story of the healing of blind Bartimaeus at Jericho *(Mark 10:46–52)*, becomes, in *Matthew (20:29–34)*, simply the healing of **two** nameless blind men. By contrast with Matthew, although Luke omits Bartimaeus' name, he faithfully reproduces Mark's detail. In *Matthew*, Jesus heals **two** Gadarene madmen *(8:28–34)* but omits some of the conversation with them, in contrast to Mark's account of 'Legion' *(5:1–20)*. Only Matthew records the earlier incident in Jesus' ministry, when two blind men, coming to the house where Jesus was staying, were healed *(9:27–31)* and as Jesus left the house, he also healed a dumb demoniac *(9:32–34)*.

Mark's memorable story of the healing of the deaf mute *(7:31–37)* becomes in *Matthew* simply the healings of 'the lame, blind, dumb, crippled and many other sufferers; they put them down at his feet and he healed them' *(15:29–31)*.

If the Apostle Matthew were the author he would not need to use Mark as his framework and his gospel would be full of eye-witness accounts.

Two further points must be considered:

(1) Although this gospel was not written by him, Matthew may perhaps have collected the religious and moral teaching material which is found here and in Luke's gospel. Speculation about this material has led scholars to hypothesise a possible document known as 'Quelle', meaning source, or **'Q'** or simply **The Sayings of Jesus**. Eusebius quotes Papias (ca. AD 150) as saying of the Apostle Matthew 'So then, Matthew compiled the Oracles in the Hebrew language; but everyone interpreted them as they were able'. Most scholars agree that the first gospel was written in Greek, not translated from a Hebrew or Aramaic original. It includes quotations from the Greek Old Testament (the **Septuagint**) which version was used by non-Palestinian, i.e. Hellenistic Jews. This knowledge, therefore, rules out the gospel as being the 'oracles' spoken of by Papias.

In Septuagint usage, an 'oracle' denoted God's word for his people, usually conveyed by prophetic inspiration. 'Q', therefore, could have been the work of the Apostle Matthew: the collection of 'Sayings' would have been in Aramaic, the language Jesus spoke: the word 'interpreted' could mean 'translated', so that Papias' words could mean that various people translated the original Aramaic into Greek as best they could

Aramaic was the common language of Palestine, although the synagogue services would be conducted in Hebrew. Since Jesus quotes from the Old Testament in his teaching, he may have known Hebrew well. He was able to make a brilliant summary of the whole law and debate with the scribes about it. Greek was the universal language of the Empire, although Latin was used for official purposes. Jesus may have known some Latin and Greek and he was able to talk to Pontius Pilate. But Jesus would speak in Aramaic and he taught the crowds of people who followed him everywhere by way of parable, allegory, metaphor and epigram. More often than not as we have seen, his words were in poetic form, very like the 'oracles' of the Old Testament prophets. He engaged in controversy with the religious leaders for he was intent on seeking the inner meaning of God's will for his people: he often downgraded scribal oral tradition: 'In this way by your tradition, handed down among you, you make God's word null and void' (*Mark 7:13*). He also taught his disciples in private. We can well imagine, therefore, that these three elements in his teaching were remembered, written down and collected at an early stage to be used as a teaching manual in the life of the Christian community. The arrangement may have been chronological, and/or by topic or verbal link.

The passages usually assigned to 'Q' are:

The mission of John Baptist, the baptism and temptations of Jesus.

The Sermon on the Mount (*Matthew*) and the Sermon on the Plain (*Luke*).

John Baptist's message from prison and Jesus' tribute to him.

The disciples' missionary tour, the centurion's servant, various parables, the lament over Jerusalem and the Coming of the Son of Man.

There was no Passion narrative in Q.

(2) There is other material in Matthew's gospel not found elsewhere and collectively known as **M**. It consists of Matthew's birth and infancy stories, certain parables and teaching (in the Sermon on the Mount), further detail about Jesus' last days in Jerusalem and his resurrection narrative. But perhaps the most controversial material in *Matthew*, is what appears to be a collection of **Christian 'proof texts'** from the Jewish scriptures. Through these Matthew tries to prove that the major events in Jesus' life and ministry were the fulfilment of Old Testament prophecy. Important though these 'proof texts' may have been for those first Christian Jews who suffered hardship, rejection and persecution from their fellow Jews, they have had unfortunate repercussions for later readership. For example:

Joseph was very concerned when he discovered that his betrothed Mary was pregnant. In a dream, he was reassured by an angelic visitation which told him not to be afraid and to take Mary home to be his wife, for the child in her womb had been conceived by the Holy Spirit. This son, to be called Jesus, was to save his people from their sins. Then the passage concludes 'All this happened in order to fulfil what the Lord delared through the prophet: "A

71

virgin will conceive and bear a son, and he shall be called Immanuel," a name which means "God is with us" ' *(1:18–25)*. The quotation is from Isaiah, 'The Lord of his own accord will give you a sign; it is this: A young woman is with child, and she will give birth to a son and call him Immanuel' *(7:14)*. The REB translation is taken from the Hebrew text, where it is clear that Isaiah in no way means or even implies a virgin conception. Isaiah gave a message of reassurance to the king Ahaz. Israel would be delivered from her enemies. The 'sign' to be given was that by the time the child was born the danger would be past, so that his mother would name him Immanuel. This passage had no Jewish messianic connotations. In other words, it has been both misused and misinterpreted by Matthew.

The phrase 'All this happened in order to fulfil what the Lord declared through the prophets' occurs 12 times throughout the gospel, followed by an Old Testament passage or illustration – *1:23; 2:6,15,18,23; 4:15–16; 8:17; 12:18–21; 13:35; 21:4–6; 26:56; 27:9–10*. While it is not appropriate to go through them all in detail, the example above illustrates that the quotation can be quite misleading, even if given in good faith. One quotation; 'He shall be called a Nazarene' *(2:23)*, cannot be traced at all, unless it is associated in some way with the Hebrew word 'nezer' meaning 'branch'.

In conclusion, we do not know who wrote the first gospel, but from its content he was clearly a Jewish Christian who composed his gospel with *Mark* and 'Q' as his basis, contributing his own material from his own sources.

At the time it was written the Christian community seems to have developed its own organisation and discipline as shown particularly in *ch. 18:15–17*; 'If your brother does wrong, go and take the matter up with him, strictly between yourselves. If he listens to you, you have won your brother over. But if he will not listen, take one or two others with you, so that every case may be settled on the evidence of two or three witnesses. If he refuses to listen to them, report the matter to the congregation; and if he will not listen to the congregation, then treat him as you would a pagan or tax-collector'. This suggests a date perhaps around AD 80, especially as in *28:19* a late form of baptism is used: 'baptise them in the name of the Father and the Son and the Holy Spirit' whereas in *Acts*, Peter offers his listeners baptism 'in the name of Jesus, the Messiah' *(2:38)*.

On the other hand we cannot be categorical about date but only about order. All we can say with certainty is that it was written after *Mark* and perhaps after *Luke*.

72

Purpose and Characteristics

1. Matthew clearly presents **Jesus as the Jewish Messiah** and the opening words of his gospel are 'The genealogy of Jesus Christ, son of David, son of Abraham' *(1:1)*. He starts with Abraham and ends with Joseph, 'the husband of Mary, who gave birth to Jesus called Messiah' *(v.16)*. The incongruity of tracing Jesus' descent through Joseph does not seem to strike him, as technically Jesus became Joseph's legal son, after his marriage to Mary. His genealogy answers questions about Jesus' identity – he was son of David (a title which Matthew uses in his gospel – *9:27, 12:23; 15:22*) therefore heir to the royal house, and son of Abraham, therefore inheritor of God's promise *(Genesis 22:18; 12:1–3)*. And in *v.21* where he states that Mary conceived through the Holy Spirit, he identifies Jesus as the son of God.

2. The first five books in the Old Testament, known as the Law, or the **Torah** are the heart and kernel of the Jewish faith. Traditionally they have always been ascribed to Moses, the greatest figure in the Old Testament. Matthew believed that Jesus was greater than Moses and that his message formed a new and higher law. He therefore arranged the teaching of Jesus into five sections, drawing attention to the parallel with the Mosaic books. The endings of these sections are marked by the phrase 'When Jesus had finished this discourse' *(7:28, cf. also 11:1; 13:53; 19:1; 26:1)*. Various titles have been suggested for each section, attempting to summarise the theme but it is impossible to know what the author had in mind. What is certain, I believe, is that Jesus himself did not deliver long sermons. Matthew's arrangement, therefore, is in accordance with his plan to present Jesus' life and ministry as the new law. At the conclusion of a series of parables, Matthew gives us *(13:51–52)* the Jewish-Christian ideal as embodied in his gospel. If a rabbi becomes a disciple of Jesus, he has both the riches of his ancestral faith and the new insights of the longed-for Messiah. '"Have you understood all this?" he (Jesus) asked; and they answered "yes". So he said to them, "When, therefore, a teacher of the law has become a learner in the kingdom of Heaven, he is like a householder who can produce from his store things new and old".'

3. Jewish Christians were much persecuted by their fellow Jews who regarded them as renegades, so we find in Matthew's gospel strong anti-Jewish feeling. For example, after the parable of the Wicked Tenants, Matthew adds a sentence attributed to Jesus, which is a further condemnation of the Jewish religious leadership: 'Therefore, I tell you the kingdom of God will be taken away from you, and given to a nation that yields the proper fruit' *(21:43)*.

We know from Mark that Jesus was very critical of certain characteristics exhibited by the Pharisees and their scribes, mainly spiritual pride and too much attention to outward instead of inward observance of the Law. Since both *Luke (11:37–52)* and *Matthew (23:1–36)* include further indictments by Jesus, their common material must originate in '*Q*', but the backbone of *Matthew 23* is found nowhere else. This chapter makes terrible reading and reflects the suffering of Jewish Christians in Matthew's own time rather than that of Jesus. Paul and his contemporaries had personal experience of flogging, hounding from city to city and, in some cases, even crucifixion.

Luke's pro-Roman sympathies influenced his presentation of the trial and death of Jesus – Pilate three times attempts to release Jesus: *(Luke 23:14–16; 20:22)* and it is Herod's soldiers who mock Jesus, not the Romans. But Matthew's anti-Jewish sentiments are clearly demonstrated by the paragraph found only in his gospel: 'When Pilate saw that he was getting nowhere, and that there was danger of a riot, he took water and washed his hands in full view of the crowd. "My hands are clean of this man's blood," he declared. "See to that yourselves." With one voice the people cried, "His blood be on us and on our children"' *(27:24–25)*. How often has that cry been echoed down centuries of Jewish persecution by Christians? The tone of Matthew's gospel and the authority with which the church invested it helps explain, but certainly not excuse, such attitudes.

4. There is some internal evidence in the gospel to suggest that it was written after a disastrous Jewish war against Rome and the fall of Jerusalem in AD 70. The author is undoubtedly very interested in rewards and punishments, the crisis of the times caused by Jewish rejection of their Messiah, the belief in the Second Coming of Christ and the final Judgement. Material found in *Mark* and '*Q*' on these subjects, has been considerably expanded in *Matthew*. He also includes awful warnings about the fate of those who reject Jesus. 'But those who were born to the kingdom (i.e. Jewish) will be thrown out into the dark, where there will be wailing and grinding of teeth' *(8:13)*. 'That is how it will be at the end of time. The angels will go out, and they will separate the wicked from the good, and throw them into the blazing furnace, where there will be wailing and grinding of teeth' *(13:50)*.

Sometimes Matthew adds a note to a parable which changes its whole tone. The story of the Unmerciful Servant *(18:21–35)* tells of a king who forgave a dishonest servant his huge debt, only to find later that this man had mercilessly pursued a colleague and thrown him into prison because he could not repay a trifling sum. The king was very angry because his servant should have learnt from his master's generosity. 'Ought you not to have shown mercy to your fellow-servant just as I showed mercy to you?' The fate of the wretched servant was to be handed over to the torturers. Yet Matthew has added 'That is how my heavenly Father will deal with you, unless you each forgive your brother from your hearts'. This threatening attitude is not characteristic of Jesus' teaching at all. Jesus' positive way of dealing with forgiveness is stated in his prayer 'Forgive us the wrong we have done, as we have forgiven those who have wronged us' (6:12). We can not be forgiven unless we are in the state of mind which is also ready to forgive.

Another footnote of Matthew's alters the parable of the Labourers in the Vineyard (20:1–16). A landowner employed men at various times during the day to work in his vineyard. When they were paid they all received the same wage much to the annoyance of those men who had toiled away throughout the hot sun and felt they were being unfairly treated. The owner makes the point that the wage agreed upon had been paid and that he had a right to do what he wanted with his own money. The parable had nothing to do with trade union regulations but simply with the central point that the love of God for all his children is so great that it overflows to everyone regardless of any individual's merits. Matthew's addition is 'So the last will be first and the first last' – but this makes a nonsense of the central point of the parable. He was presumably thinking of the Christian community having pre-eminence over the old Israel, but he had missed the essential meaning of Jesus' words.

Matthew ends Jesus' fifth and final discourse with three majestic parables which are open to several interpretations, but which for Matthew point to the Second Coming of the Messiah and Final Judgement. He places these parables after his apocalyptic chapter.

(a) The Ten Girls (25:1–13). We are not familiar with the marriage customs of Jesus' day, but apparently the bride waited for the groom to come to her home, the wedding party was then escorted through the streets to the groom's house where the wedding feast was held. It is not clear whether the 10 girls in the story were bridesmaids or simply friends of the bride. They went to meet the groom with their lamps but had quite a long wait. Five of the girls had made provision for this and had gone supplied with some spare oil. The other five had not thought so far ahead, therefore when the groom did come, at midnight, their lamps were going out. They hurried to buy some more oil and so missed the arrival of the groom, the entire wedding party, and were quite shut out of the celebrations. In biblical symbolism, the feast is the kingdom, and the bridegroom, the Messiah. The bride does not come into the story at all! In the context of Jesus' own life, the parable could be a warning to the disciples to be prepared for Jesus' return, but it is more likely that they should be ready for the impending crisis. In the context of Matthew's time, the girls represent the waiting Christian community who are expecting the Second Coming of their Lord. Those who are ready receive the kingdom, the others are left outside.

The sharp division between those who are accepted into the kingdom and those who are left outside is found in other parables in this gospel, such as the wheat and the darnel or weeds *(13:24–30)* and the marriage feast *(22:1–14)*. This division, however, does not seem compatible with the stories of the lost sheep and the lost coin *(Luke 15:1–10,* also in *Matthew 18:12–14).*

Any relevant lesson for today in the Ten Girls story, must be based on life's experience. It is important to be alert to every opportunity, because it may not occur again. Being open and receptive to the promptings of the Spirit can even sometimes prepare us for the unexpected.

(b) The Talents *(25:14–30).* The central point of this well known story is the same as that made by Jesus in Mark's gospel *(4:25).* If you do not use, you lose. Perhaps Jesus was thinking of the priceless religious heritage of the Jewish nation, which the religious leaders did not seem to be willing to share with the rest of humanity. Perhaps he was thinking about its application to the individual. The man who did nothing with his one bag of gold, made the excuse: 'Master, I knew you to be a hard man: you reap where you have not sown, you gather where you have not scattered, so I was afraid, and I went and hid your gold in the ground. Here it is – you have what belongs to you'. The interesting point in the story is that the master did not deny the description and indeed this is how we can experience life itself. It does not always treat us fairly; nevertheless we have to make the most of what we have been given. The lazy servant did not even put his master's money on deposit to gain some interest whilst he was away, his punishment was to have the one talent taken away from him and given to the servant who originally had five bags. The rewards for both the other servants who had respectively doubled what they had been given, was to be put in charge of something much bigger and 'to share your master's joy'. Matthew had added a final comment: 'As for the useless servant, throw him out into the dark, where there will be wailing and grinding of teeth'. This does not in fairness fit the parable for the punishment has already been given, but it is in keeping with Matthew's views of eternal damnation.

(c) The Last Judgement *(25:31–46).* In this story, the Son of Man is the judge, later called the king. The king's father is God. The scene is the final winding up of history and present are all the nations of the earth. The record of every individual is already known so that separation between the good and the bad is clear just as a Judaean shepherd would easily divide his flock into sheep and goats, which were herded together during the day but separated at night. The basis of the judgement is how a person has reacted to another's need 'For when I was hungry, you gave me food; when thirsty, you gave me drink; when I was a stranger, you took me into your home; when naked, you clothed me; when I was ill, you came to my help; when in prison, you visited me. . . . Truly I tell you: anything you did for one of my brothers here, however insignificant, you did it for me'. Some people interpret 'brother' to mean specifically a disciple of Jesus, for Jesus had described all those who heard the word of God and did it, as his spiritual family. Probably this is Matthew's own interpretation for this view has come down to us through the centuries and is still held in certain quarters of the Christian church. But to define 'brother' so narrowly is, I believe, a travesty of Jesus' intention and universal relevance. Those who hear the word of God and act upon it are those who are motivated by compassionate truth, consideration and respect for others, even if they know nothing of Jesus himself. The kingdom of God, according to Jesus, is the inner reign of Love in a person's heart and life. In the parable of the Good Samaritan it is the compassionate man of a despised race who reaches out to the need of another and treats him as a neighbour. Mother Teresa of Calcutta has said 'Every person is Christ for me, and since there is only one Jesus, that person is the only person in the world for me at that moment'. She and her sisters interpret 'brother' as any member of the human race, whether man or woman, who is desperately in need.

We need now to sum up the curiously ambivalent picture of Jesus, with which Matthew's gospel presents us. On the one hand we have challenging, cryptic and provocative sayings and parables. All that the document 'Q' gives us is early, genuine and vital to our picture of this extraordinary man and we shall assume that the temptations of Jesus and most of the Sermon on the Mount (to be discussed in the next chapter) comes from 'Q'. But side by side with this breadth and wisdom, there is the rather parochial, even vindictive turn of phrase and the unreal wonderworker who produces a coin in a fish's mouth in order to pay the tax for the upkeep of the Temple (17:24–27). Whatever the origins of this latter story, I cannot credit that it was an actual episode in Jesus' life, especially given his views on money!

All the evidence suggests that Matthew is writing to represent the interests of a small, isolated Jewish Christian community, living in a hostile climate of opinion or even enduring actual persecution. Its members were entirely convinced that Jesus was the Messiah and hoped against all odds, that they would be vindicated by God at the Second Coming. The later date of this gospel is shown by the fact that the word 'church' (Greek 'ecclesia') appears here and nowhere else: 'You are Peter, the Rock; and on this rock I will build my church, and the powers of death shall never conquer it. I will give you the keys of the kingdom of Heaven; what you forbid on earth shall be forbidden in heaven, and what you allow on earth shall be allowed in heaven' *(16:18)*.

It is in this gospel that Peter is given such pre-eminence and that exclusive salvation authority is vested in the Apostles. This is out of keeping with what we read of Jesus in the other gospels.

I feel it has been a tragedy for Christendom, that the first gospel was considered definitive and treated as such for centuries by the Church Fathers. Even today there are some scholars who would still place it earlier than Mark. It must carry a major responsibility for hardened attitudes towards the Jews, and for a belief in predetermination because everything of significance in the gospel was a fulfilment of Jewish scriptures, including Judas' betrayal of Jesus and eventual suicide *(27:9–10)*. It has also led to the supreme authority vested in Peter and his successors to forbid or allow for eternity, the dreadful over-simplified division between the good and the bad, the emphasis on rewards and punishment and the threat of eternal torment. Perhaps, more than anything, I regret the tragic blurring in *Matthew* of the actual humanity of Jesus himself, which was so clearly emphasised in the earlier gospel, *Mark*.

The greatness of Matthew's gospel probably lies in the way the author has arranged his material, especially in the Sermon on the Mount, and has added some marvellously powerful parables and sayings of Jesus from his own source. But these have to be seen in the context of the writer's own time and the faith and courage of those beleaguered Jewish Christians who yet declared that Jesus of Nazareth was the long awaited Messiah. We have also to remember that Matthew begins his story with the visit of the completely non-Jewish wise men and ends with the risen Jesus, the Christ, bidding his disciples to go to all nations and make them his disciples. The gospel ends with the words 'I will be with you always, to the end of time'.

CHAPTER TWELVE

Matthew's gospel, part II

The Temptations of Jesus (4:1–11)

The record of Jesus' experiences in the wilderness is found only in Luke's and Matthew's gospels so it is always assumed to be part of the 'Q' document. At some time Jesus must have told his friends the detail of his own mental conflict about the kind of Messiah he would become. He expressed the various options open to him in poetic symbols and pictorial imagery which his companions would readily understand. But the significance and universal application of these temptations is profound for they open up the whole issue of the right and wrong uses of power.

At Jesus' baptism, he had received inner confirmation about his mission. He had been called to 'bring in the kingdom of God' into the lives of his own people and beyond. He went away into the wilderness to think through the implications of his special charge. Matthew represents this action of Jesus as being 'led by the Spirit . . . to be tempted by the devil'. The Old Testament had a very realistic and natural concept of spiritual fulfilment. God's promise to Abraham at the beginning of the biblical story was 'I shall make you into a great nation; I shall bless you and make your name so great that it will be used in blessings: those who bless you, I shall bless; those who curse you, I shall curse. All the people on earth will wish to be blessed as you are blessed' *(Genesis 12:2,3).* So popular expectation of the Messiah was that he would liberate his people from the Roman yoke, establish his people 'in possession of the cities of their enemies' *(Genesis 22:18)* and above all bring in an age of prosperity and plenty. To the deprived and poor of Israel, the prospect of the Messianic feast was a cherished idea.

The first temptation of Jesus was therefore to devote all his time and energy to the physical and material needs of his compatriots. Any move to alleviate poverty would bring great popularity. Having spent time fasting,

79

he would have been very consious of his own hunger. This was self-imposed, but what about all those who were short of food through no fault of their own? How could he help them? This messianic option was expressed in the form of the tempter saying 'If you are the Son of God, tell the stones to become bread'. But Jesus knew that his personal mission was on a more profound level, even though it was necessary to meet people's basic physical needs. His answer therefore came from *Deuteronomy*, 'Man is not to live by bread alone, but on every word that comes from the mouth of God' *(8:3)*.

In the latter part of our century, terrible famines have been experienced especially by the peoples of Africa. Their plight has been exacerbated by civil war. We know that there are the material means within the world community to feed the hungry; only the moral will and commitment are lacking. Jesus' **own** priority was to bring about a change in human nature, although he did what he could to meet immediate needs as he met them. Dire consequences, however, have arisen out of humanity's spiritual and moral aridity.

The second temptation in *Matthew* is placed third by Luke. In imagination, Jesus seems to have thought of himself as standing on the parapet of the Temple, the heart of his nation's faith. The temptation was twofold: first, to give people absolute proof of his messiahship by producing some overwhelming sign; second, to prove to himself the truth of his inner vision at his baptism, asking divine support for his manifestation of power. 'If you are the Son of God' said the tempter, 'throw yourself down; for scripture says "He will put his angels in charge of you, and they will support you in their arms, for fear you should strike your foot against a stone"' *(Psalm 91:11–12)*. Jesus' answer to this is again from *Deuteronomy* 'You are not to put the Lord your God to the test' *(6:16)*. He saw that testing God in such a way was really a refusal to trust him. In modern terms we can see this second conflict as a refusal to use brainwashing techniques, propaganda or advertising in order to manipulate people or win their support. We experience the power of the media every day. The brilliant political communicator can win a great deal of support through the media. But in the end, there is more to human beings than gullibility. We learn by experience and we remember unfulfilled promises; people power is one of the most fascinating movements to emerge in our present time. We have to be true to our own personal convictions and we actually test our inner certainties by being faithful to them. Jesus' ultimate faith in God as his loving Father was vindicated, even if he had to go through terrible experiences to arrive at the other side.

The words '**If** you are the son of God . . .' also reveal Jesus' own humanity; he was, of course, prey to self doubt at times. Self-awareness is often accompanied by self-doubt but through the honest and humbling process of self-appraisal, conviction grows that we are on the right path. Jesus must have experienced this very acute temptation to seek obvious divine confirmation that he was God's son in a special sense, especially in the latter days of his life.

The third temptation in *Matthew* is presented as a visionary mountain top experience in which Jesus was shown all the kingdoms of the world. They were presumably pagan, for Satan offered him their allegiance on easy terms: 'All these,' the tempter said, 'I will give you, if you will only fall down and do me homage.' This must have represented the way of compromise. Jesus was tempted to use the evil means of armed rebellion against Rome to achieve Jewish liberation. Many believed that the only way to regain national sovereignty was by military force. The Zealots tried this continually and failed. All the evidence shows that if Jesus had decided to become a rebel leader he would have had an immense following. He did have one Zealot disciple and in the end he was crucified on a treasonable offence. Jesus' answer again comes from *Deuteronomy* 'Out of my sight, Satan! Scripture says, "You shall do homage to the Lord your God and worship him alone"' (6:13).
History has shown how men and women can become corrupted by power, especially if they attempt to take short cuts and adopt morally doubtful means to achieve their goals. The incorruptible are those who have an inner higher allegiance, whether moral or spiritual, which is more important to them than the achievement of immediate results.

Three further points: First, all these temptations represented something very real in the life of Jesus and cropped up again during the course of his ministry; the demand for a sign is an obvious example. Second, he drew strength and help in resolving his conflict, from the book of *Deuteronomy*. This was reputedly Moses' farewell sermon to the Israelites as they were about to go forward to take Canaan, their promised land. Perhaps Jesus was thinking of his namesake and great predecessor, Joshua, who established the Israelites in Canaan and was comparing his own mission in leading his people to understand the true nature of the kingdom. Third, he rejected the popular conceptions of messiahship and chose instead to be, above all, God's servant. From his use of Old Testament quotations throughout his ministry, it is obvious that the Servant Songs of Isaiah (42:1–4; 49:1–6; 50:4–9; 52:13 – 53:12) meant a great deal to him. They picture the suffering servant of God, possibly a single individual, or perhaps the faithful remnant of Israel. 'He was pierced for our transgressions, crushed for our iniquities; the chastisement he bore restored us to health and by his wounds we are healed' (53:5). The vicarious suffering of this

81

servant had application beyond the boundaries of Israel. Therefore Jesus himself chose the way of sacrificial love, demonstrating by his life and teaching the inner truths of the kingdom, but giving to others the dignity of individual choice. Only so could they grow to become responsible human beings.

The Sermon on the Mount *(5:1 – 7:29)*

It is of course impossible to deal adequately in a few pages, with this great section of Matthew's gospel. Nevertheless, I think it is worth while to highlight several important facets of this collection of Jesus' teachings. As it now stands in the gospel, Jesus supposedly delivered this sermon on a mountain, as did Moses, when on Mount Sinai he delivered the law to the Israelites *(Exodus 19–20)*. The sermon is addressed primarily to the disciples because in it Jesus is saying – theṣe are the qualities you must possess if you are truly to be citizens of the kingdom.

(a) The Beatitudes *(5:3–12)*. These extraordinary eight or nine statements are not 'pie in the sky' or a piously idealistic view of what human nature might become. Jesus was a realist, not an idealist in the modern sense of the term. The beatitudes – how blest or how happy – portray a quality of character, an inward source of energy, from which, Jesus positively asserted, inevitable results would follow.

'Blessed are the poor in spirit; the kingdom of Heaven is theirs.' The poverty of which Jesus is talking, is surely the moral and spiritual aridity mentioned above. To be self-aware enough to know our need, means that there is a chance of that need being met. The presence of the kingdom is the acknowledgement of the supremacy of love in a person's life. It is the converse of the self-righteous Pharisee who prayed in the temple. He was unaware of any lack in himself so he received nothing.

'Blessed are the sorrowful; they shall find consolation.' The capacity for suffering is also the capacity for joy. To suffer in the cause of love, either through sensitivity to others' pain or through our own, can be a growing point in loving. To share in the grief and rejoicing of others bonds us together in loving relationships. If we are indifferent to others, we shall know neither sorrow nor joy.

'Blessed are the gentle; they shall have the earth for their possession.' This seems quite contrary to the accepted wisdom of the world for surely it is the aggressive, the ruthless and the self-assertive who are successful. But in what do they succeed? Jesus saw true humility as a sign of strength because this quality enables us to look at and respect others as people in their own right. This is the true perspective on life. For Jesus also, greatness was measured by service to others (*Mark 10:44*), not by being served. And the result of gentleness is that we can be trusted not to exploit, ravage and destroy the earth; it will then be really ours. Unless humanity as a whole can learn this fundamental truth of cause and effect, our planet home will cease to sustain life as we know it and will be no one's possession.

'Blessed are those who hunger and thirst to see right prevail; they shall be satisfied.' Jesus' imagery shows clearly his passionate concern for justice and harmony. Experience does not always seem to confirm this statement for many have died in grief at not seeing the cause of justice realised. But Jesus does not say that people will see a just cause vindicated in their lifetime. His own work still continues centuries after his death. Jesus was probably talking about the inner peace which can come from having fought for a righteous cause whatever the outcome.

'Blessed are those who show mercy; mercy shall be shown to them.' The need to forgive, was one of Jesus' most innovative themes and was applicable not only in our relationship with God, but with everyone else. The word mercy can also mean to show compassion to those who have no claim upon us as in the parable of the Good Samaritan. It can be linked to the theme of judging others but its reciprocal nature is also important.

'Blessed are those whose hearts are pure; they shall see God.' In Old Testament thought the majesty of God was so great that a mere mortal could not survive an encounter with his glory. Moses was the exception for 'The Lord used to speak to Moses face to face, as one man speaks to another' (*Exodus 33:11*). For Jesus, however, the inner harmony which came from a sense of union with the Father, was the natural outcome of a certain way of life. 'The pure in heart' are those people who are uncluttered by mixed motives, clear and single-minded in their devotion to God or the highest good. They are able to see and apprehend their objective by whatever name it is known.

'Blessed are the peace-makers; they shall be called God's children.' To be a true peace-maker or reconciler requires qualities of love, truth, patience and the ability to see all sides of a situation, which have been associated with divinity. It takes the compassionate, strong and mature person to mediate, for reconciliation is not corrupting compromise, nor is it peace at any price. Jesus did not tolerate exploitation when he saw it. He cleared out of the Court of the Gentiles all who were exploiting others. We are not called to submit to injustice and oppression, but to work to turn these things into their opposites. And our efforts are blessed by strength and grace.

'Blessed are those who are persecuted in the cause of right; the Kingdom of Heaven is theirs.' Supporters of a just cause can experience the enmity of others whose self-regarding aims are not so noble. In our own time, prisoners of conscience who have not resorted to violence to advance their views, and who yet have been imprisoned, tortured or killed, are exactly the kind of people Jesus was talking about. In the next verse he reminded his disciples of the fate of the prophets before them. Even so the inner reality of the kingdom with its peace and joy, can be indeed a possession for those who endure.

This section ends with Jesus telling his disciples that they are to be like salt to the world and shed light among their fellows 'so that when they see the good you do, they may give praise to your Father in heaven' (*vs. 13–16*).

(b) The New Law (*5:21–48*). Jesus did not legislate on every detail of life, his genius lay in giving vivid examples of how people behave when motivated by love. For Jesus, the inner disposition was supremely important as it was this that gave rise to eventual action. In the following six examples, Jesus first states the old law, then he adds his comment.

First: murder (*Exodus 20:13*) and its punishment: when Jesus then points out that anger or hatred should also be condemned, he implies that these are the feelings which lead a person to desperate actions. (Matthew has then added two further statements which deal with the necessity of reconciliation before worship.)

Second: adultery (*Exodus 20:14*): But Jesus points out that it is the presence of lust which is at the root of adultery. The difference between lust and love is not a matter of sexual passion, but the way in which the other person is regarded. Lust looks on the other as an object to satisfy desire. But love sees the other as a person to be respected and reverenced in their own right.

Third: divorce (*Deuteronomy 24:1–4*). In Mark's gospel Jesus discussed this whole question with a group of Pharisees, not only emphasising the original nature of the marriage relationship, but also placing men and women on a footing of equality. Here he adds that only 'unchastity' is a valid reason for divorce. By implication, if the couple have extra marital relations or cease to regard each other with the depth of feeling which is involved in this act of sexual union, then the relationship has so changed its essence that divorce may be the only possible outcome.

Fourth: vows and oaths (*Exodus 20:7* and *Leviticus 19:12*, which dealt with perjury). Jesus felt that oath taking was a product of evil intention. For the honest person an oath was quite unnecessary.

Fifth: revenge. The Mosaic regulation of 'an eye for an eye', i.e. strict justice (*Exodus 21:23–25, Leviticus 24:20, Deuteronomy 19:20*) was a great improvement on the earlier right to repay injury with interest (in *Genesis 4:15*, vengeance was sevenfold). But Jesus cancels out revenge altogether. The active spirit of love will not be overcome by evil. He gives three extreme

84

examples of behaviour denoting great inner strength. When someone slaps your right cheek, turn the other: when someone takes your shirt, give your coat as well (as the average Israelite only had two articles of clothing, this would leave him naked!): when press-ganged by the state courier to provide transport for one mile, go two instead. We must not make the mistake of a literal interpretation which would rob these thumbnail sketches of their power. The whole point is that we should not respond to wrong doing, bullying, theft, or oppression in like manner. Jesus was certainly not passive. He himself did not condone the exploitation of the Court of the Gentiles in the Temple. He acted to right the wrong situation. Injustice, oppression and violence must be dealt with but not by evil methods, otherwise we become part of the evil process itself and the situation escalates.

Sixth: love (*Leviticus 19:18*, which does not specifically say 'hate your enemies'). To the Jews, 'neighbour' meant fellow Israelite; they would feel justifed in hating the Romans. Jesus, however, believed in and practised a compassionate response to friend and foe alike. This required a quite exceptional quality of selflessness. Later in the Sermon *(7:12)* he gave his disciples the golden rule 'Always treat others as you would like them to treat you', which sums up his teaching on love.

(c) The New Worship *(6:1–18)*. Again Jesus concentrates on the importance of inner motivation rather than outward show. He gives three examples which vividly differentiate between those who act for the sake of other people's good opinion and those who do things in complete sincerity.

One: Charity or almsgiving. Hypocrites are generous in support of this or that good cause, not because they particularly care about it, but because they want 'to win the praise of others'. 'Truly I tell you,' says Jesus, 'they have their reward already.' In other words they get what they are paying for! On the other hand, the giver who really cares, does so without anyone else knowing about it. The fact that Jesus says 'your Father who sees what is done in secret will reward you' does not mean literally that we are to give because we will be rewarded in heaven. If so, we are not much better than the hypocrite. On the contrary, the true generosity which acts in response to need brings its own fulfilment.

Two: Prayer. The devout Jew practised a number of public acts of worship as well as private devotions. Apparently it was not difficult to gain a reputation for piety, if one wished to do so. But the quality of real prayer was of a different nature. 'When you pray, go into a room by yourself, shut the door, and pray to your Father who is in secret; and your Father who sees what is done in secret will reward you.' For Jesus, prayer meant profoundly personal interior conversation with the source of his being. The practice of this deep communication brings its own enrichment and self-enlightenment; as God knows our needs, we do not need to repeat them endlessly but by articulating them in prayer, we may see them more clearly and truly.

In Luke's gospel Jesus answers the disciples' question about prayer by giving them a pattern to follow, known to us now as The Lord's Prayer. Matthew's version of this prayer is given in the context of Jesus' discussion on right and wrong motivation in worship. We are so familiar with this prayer that it can almost become non-effective, but it is a concise statement of a particular attitude to life. It begins with Jesus' belief in the Fatherhood of God; we must honour him as such, particularly by working for the coming of the kingdom both as the present active reign of Love in people's hearts and minds, and also as a future universal hope. Second, the prayer recognises our personal and corporate needs at every level – bread, forgiveness (i.e. mutual relationships of compassion) and suffering. The words 'do not put us to the test' must not be taken literally as if God deliberately tests faith, for this is not at all the function of Love. Because of his particular culture and religious background, Jesus continually personalises the facts of our existence but we must not allow this to confuse us about the truth of his witness. As human beings, we find that life itself repeatedly tests us, only so can we learn and grow. The prayer asks that we may have strength to overcome any eventuality which life places in our path.

Three: Fasting. The Pharisees and the disciples of John Baptist fasted regularly and were seen to do so by others. The Pharisees criticised Jesus because he did not particularly encourage his disciples to follow this religious discipline. But for Jesus, fasting and all other such exercises in self-control, must be done for the right motives and in strict privacy so that other people were not necessarily aware of them. Only so could such disciplines achieve their real purpose of spiritual growth and development.

(d) The Two Ways (6:19–34). Matthew has collected together four sayings in which Jesus sharply contrasts two differing attitudes to life.

Earthly and heavenly treasure: The impermanence and anxiety associated with worldly wealth is contrasted with the durability of spiritual resources.

Light and darkness: A healthy eye is an essential to physical sight. A diseased eye plunges the body into darkness. 'If then the only light you have is darkness, how great a darkness that will be.' Jesus' powerful poetic imagery portrays the dense spiritual blindness caused by false perspectives.

God and money: It is impossible to serve two masters adequately: in what do we really trust – spiritual and moral values or material prosperity? It is, of course, possible to enjoy relative prosperity and retain one's moral integrity; Jesus means that we must have a clear scale of priorities. If we place total security in wealth, it blinds our judgement on ultimate values. Trust and anxiety: Jesus was not an ascetic nor did he recommend a fine disregard for proper future provision. He is here urging his disciples not to be over anxious about things which might be unalterable, such as a person's height! In beautiful imagery he shows his love of the natural world and through it stresses the need to have a proper sense of perspective in all things. By cultivating a certain detachment and freedom from worry, we can gain a sense of harmony and well being.

(e) Right judgement *(7 : 1–11)*: We need to have loving, honest, reciprocal and non-judgemental relationships with each other. 'First take the plank out of your own eye, and then you will see clearly to take the speck out of your brother's.' In the difficult saying about 'pearls to the pigs' Jesus may be stressing the need to discriminate wisely. If people are offered something quite inappropriate to their particular state of mind and situation, they may not only reject the gift but actually hate the giver. If we are truly sensitive, we treat people as distinct individuals and assess correctly what is needed.

Jesus had complete faith that God always responded to his children's needs. Hence his words 'ask, seek, knock', and his comparison between God and the caring parent who wishes to answer his child's hunger: 'how much more will your heavenly Father give good things to those who ask him!' Genuine prayer is always answered but we do not always worship him 'in spirit and in truth' *(John 4 : 24)*, and therefore we are not always capable of recognising God's response.

Jesus' picture of the two gates, one narrow and difficult but leading to life, the other broad and easy but leading to destruction is difficult. It gives a stark either/or picture of life while most of us live by reasonable compromise. However, Jesus is talking about the inward journey of the soul and the intent of the will. Which way are we going? Are we walking in the company of those who seek to live compassionate, creative, honest and responsible lives, even though they may often fail, or are we walking in the opposite direction driven by greed, ruthless selfishness and total disregard for others so long as we get what we want? Although there is usually some saving grace in any one individual, however evil his/her life may be, nevertheless it is also true that the two ways of life are seemingly incompatible. The former leads eventually to the affirmation of our common humanity, the latter to self-destruction and disaster for the individual concerned and suffering for the innocent.

Jesus' teaching does include a Day of Judgement. It is possible that he visualised this as an actual event. Whether we can accept his imagery or not, we can all appreciate the fact that 'judgement' takes place throughout our lives, through the law of cause and effect in the moral sphere.

Jesus definitely warned his disciples to beware of false prophets and false disciples who can always be recognised by the quality of their lives. 'A good tree always yields sound fruit, and a poor tree bad fruit.'

Jesus' advice is always to be alert, awake and aware. It is fitting, therefore, that Matthew concludes the Sermon with the parable of the wise and foolish house builders. In countries like Israel, heavy rain can very quickly turn dry river beds into raging torrents, sweeping away sandy levels. In building, therefore, it is necessary to dig down to rocky foundations otherwise your house may be swept away at the next flood. The wise builder, says Jesus, is the one who 'hears these words of mine and acts on them'. The foolish will hear but not act. Matthew adds, somewhat needlessly perhaps, that the people were amazed at Jesus' authority so unlike the methods used by the scribes.

It is inconceivable that Jesus uttered a sermon of this dimension and depth on a single occasion. Matthew has evidently collected together, probably for teaching purposes, some of the key elements from Jesus' teaching.

CHAPTER THIRTEEN

A note on John's gospel and his presentation of Jesus

Introduction

PROBABLY THERE HAS been more written about John's gospel than on any other New Testament book. It is a powerful work of great attraction and challenge. In the present context, however, it is only possible to discuss a few essential points and to look briefly at several controversial questions in order to establish the nature and authenticity of this witness to Jesus. These questions include – who wrote the gospel, the possible background of the author, where and when it was written, its relationship with the synoptic gospels and the writer's purpose.

Authorship Traditionally, on the evidence of second and third century writers, the book was considered to be the work of John the Apostle, the son of Zebedee and brother of James. He is mentioned in Mark's gospel on many occasions and formed one of the three men closest to Jesus. The Muratori fragment which lists the scriptures acknowledged by the Roman church (c. AD 190) says 'The fourth of the Gospels was written by John, one of the disciples.'

The evidence of Irenaeus, bishop of Lyons, ca AD 170–200, is of particular interest. As a boy, Irenaeus sat at the feet of Polycarp, Bishop of Smyrna (martyred at the age of 86 in AD 155). Polycarp himself had been a personal friend of the Apostle John and others who had seen Jesus. Irenaeus says 'John, the disciple of the Lord, who leaned on his breast, himself issued the Gospel while dwelling in Ephesus'. He also adds that John lived there until the times of Trajan (AD 98).

In the gospel itself the author remains anonymous. The only specific clue to him is in *ch. 21:24* 'It is this same disciple who vouches for what has been written here. He it is who wrote it, and we know that his testimony is true'.

It is generally accepted that chapter 21 is an appendix to the gospel, but this should not necessarily detract from its merit.

Two further points:

(a) the claim of **a direct witness to events** in *ch.1:14*. 'So the Word became flesh; he made his home among us and we saw his glory'; in *ch.19:35* 'This is vouched for by an eyewitness (the stabbing of Jesus' side by a lance), whose evidence is to be trusted. He knows that he speaks the truth so that you too may believe' and in *ch. 21:24*, quoted above.

(b) relates to the **disciple whom Jesus loved**, a description which crops up three times in the gospel proper, and twice in the appendix *(21:7,20)*. In the *21:20* reference – 'Peter looked round and saw the disciple whom Jesus loved following', there is a direct link with *v.24* – 'It is this same disciple who vouches for what has been written here'.

The first of the 'beloved disciple' references occurs at the Last Supper: 'One of them, the disciple he loved, was reclining close beside Jesus. Simon Peter signalled to him to find out which one he meant' *(13:23,24)*: the second, at the crucifixion 'Seeing his mother, with the disciple whom he loved standing beside her' *(19:26)*: and the third, after the resurrection – 'She (Mary Magdalene) . . . ran to Simon Peter and the other disciple, the one whom Jesus loved' *(20:2)*.

It is reasonable to conclude that the 'beloved disciple' was one of the three men who, as indicated in Mark's gospel, were closest to Jesus. He could not have been Peter, as Peter is distinguished from him in the gospel itself (see above). It could not have been James, for James was martyred by King Herod about AD 44 (according to Josephus, the Jewish historian), years before the gospel was written. This leaves John, whose claim to be the beloved disciple is further strengthened by what appears to be deliberate personal modesty. The sons of Zebedee are not mentioned at all in the fourth gospel until the appendix *(21:2)*.

The several difficulties about the Apostle John's authorship are:

(a) John was a Galilean fisherman. Even if he had been reasonably well educated by his father, who was wealthy enough to have hired servants, would such a man be capable of producing what is considered to be a developed literary and dramatic work?

(b) If the Apostle John was the author, how does one account for the discrepancies which exist between this gospel and the other three, as for example the placing of the Cleansing of the Temple at the beginning of the ministry and the different day on which the Last Supper was held? But above all there is the strikingly different presentation of Jesus, his words and his claims about himself, as shown in the great 'I am' discourses.

In answer to the first query, the Greek phrase, 'it is he who wrote it' *(21:24)* could equally well mean 'cause to be written'. Therefore although the inspiration behind the gospel was the Apostle John, a disciple of his could have been the actual Evangelist, i.e. the writer of the gospel.

Any answer to the second question concerns the relationship between the fourth gospel and the synoptics, which is discussed fully below. But above all, the fourth gospel would seem to be a profound meditation on and interpretation of the life and teaching of Jesus as given in *Mark* and *'Q'*. Jesus' words in John's gospel, therefore, reflect this process of meditation and interpretation.

Scholars continue to debate the possibilities, but for me the most acceptable view is that the authority and witness behind the gospel is the Apostle John who was in very truth the beloved disciple, but that the actual Evangelist was a disciple of John, whose name we do not know.

2. Another controversial but important question has to do with the **authorship of the three letters** attributed to John in the New Testament (although no writer's name is given in the text) and their relationship with the author of the fourth gospel. The majority of scholars agree that a study of *1 John* suggests that the writer of this letter was most probably the author of the gospel. This was indeed the view expressed in the Muratori fragment: 'What marvel therefore if John so firmly sets forth each statement in his Epistles too, saving of himself, "What we have seen with our eyes and heard with our ears and our hands have handled, these things we have written to you"? *(cf. 1 John 1:3–4)*. For so he declared himself to be not an eye witness and a hearer only, but a writer of all the marvels of the Lord in order'. The second and third letters are very short notes. They could be by the first Epistle writer, but because the author calls himself the Elder, it is thought that they are more probably by someone else.

3. For reasons of style and content, it is almost universally agreed by modern scholars that the book of **Revelation** is **not** by the gospel writer. Indeed this opinion was also held as far back as the third century by Eusebius, who agrees with the views of Dionysius, the third century bishop of Alexandria, that the character, style and anonymity of the author of the fourth gospel, prove that he could not be the same as the John, author of Revelation, who calls himself in the book itself John the Elder. In any case, if the writer of the Apocalypse had possessed direct or indirect apostolic authority, he would certainly have used it. In fact he refers to the Apostles with the great reverence of someone distant from them: 'The city walls had 12 foundation-stones and on them were the names of the 12 apostles of the lamb' *(21:14)*. In theory, it is possible that the Apostle John's disciple was also called John and that he later became John the Elder who wrote

Revelation, but the dissimilarities between the content of the fourth gospel and *Revelation* really preclude this. We are left with the likely conclusion that the gospel and the first letter were written by the disciple of John the Apostle and under his authority, while John the Elder wrote *Letters Two* and *Three* as well as *Revelation*.

4. **Date and place of writing** From the evidence of papyri fragments we know that the gospel was circulating in Egypt early in the second century, so it must have been written at least sometime ca AD 90–100. Eusebius and other 2nd-century Christian writers believed that the gospel was written at Ephesus. Eusebius says there is some evidence to suggest two Johns lived at Ephesus: 'Since it is said both that there were two tombs at Ephesus, and that each of the two is said to be John's,' he concludes that one of them was the Apostle's and the other the Elder's – the latter being the author of *Revelation*. Eusebius also includes some extracts from the writings of Papias of Hierapolis (AD 60–130) who talks of two Johns, one of whom was the Apostle and the other the Elder. Papias 'acknowledged that he had received the discourses of the apostles from those who had been their followers, but that he was himself an actual hearer of Aristion and of John the Elder'.

John Robinson, however, saw the gospel as maturing over a period of nearly 40 years reaching culmination in the late 60s. 'It gradually took shape in meditation and preaching, in evangelism and apologetic, in worship and instruction.'

5. **Cultural background**
(a) If he were the Apostle, then the writer was an Aramaic speaking Jew, steeped in Palestinian Judaistic traditions, using his own sources for his gospel. But if he had lived many years in Ephesus he would also have known Greek culture.
(b) If he were the disciple of John the Apostle, he could well then have been a Greek speaking Jew, a Hellenist. He would have been aware and perhaps knowledgeable of Greek philosophy. Practically all the linguistic evidence suggests that the author wrote in Greek, even though he probably spoke in Aramaic.

The difficulties which have been raised about the cultural background are due to the fact that scholarship has read into the gospel all kinds of influences ranging from the Dead Sea scrolls (the work of Jewish Gnostics called the Essenes), to Platonism, Stoicism, the Hermetica (Greek mystical writings) and Gnosticism in all its forms. But Greek ideas had infiltrated throughout the Greek speaking Roman empire. The Jews of the Dispersion used the Septuagint and spoke Greek also. Philo of Alexandria, a near contemporary of Jesus, who was both a philosopher and a practising Jew, had actually attempted a syncretism of Hebrew and Greek thought. It is therefore perfectly logical (as indeed some scholars have argued) to explain both the Hebraic and Hellenistic elements of John's gospel by the author's openness to the various strands of religious language and thought which were prevalent in his day.

6. **Purpose** Scholars have posited a whole range of possible readers but as the writer is careful to translate Hebrew and Aramaic words and to explain Jewish religious practices, it would seem that John was writing for Greek speaking people. As to the author's purpose, perhaps not enough attention has been given to the simple statement found in *ch. 20:31* 'Those (i.e. the signs) written here have been recorded in order that you may believe that Jesus is the Christ, the Son of God, and that through this faith you may have life by his name'.

7. Notable characteristics

(a) His chronology: The Cleansing of the Temple occurs at the beginning of Jesus' ministry *(2:12–21)* not at the end, as in *Mark*. Jesus makes several visits to Jerusalem, not one. He has a ministry in Judaea *(3:22ff)* before the Galilean one, and a later ministry in the south *(7:10 – 11:54)* after the Galilean ministry is over. The Last Supper is held a day earlier than in *Mark*.

(b) His topography: John mentions a dozen place names not found in the Synoptics but modern archaeology has confirmed rather than dismissed his statements, especially about Southern Palestine.

(c) He does not mention various incidents recorded in the Synoptics, such as the baptism, the temptations, the transfiguration and Jesus' words at the Last Supper about his body and blood. But he alone records that John Baptist encouraged two of his own disciples to follow Jesus *(1:35–39)*, and that after the feeding of the 5,000, the people wanted to make Jesus king *(6:15)*. He tells us about Nicodemus and in that conversation we have the key words 'the spirit gives birth to the spirit' *(3:6)*. In the graphic encounter of Jesus with the Samaritan woman, another key phrase is uttered 'God is spirit and those who worship him must worship in spirit and in truth' *(4:24)*. John also recounts Jesus' ministry in Judaea *(chs. 7,9)*, the raising of Lazarus, the foot-washing, and the fact that after his arrest Jesus made an informal appearance before Annas, the former High Priest *(18:13ff)*.

(d) His theological approach: His great Prologue sets the story of Jesus beyond time: 'In the beginning the Word already was' *(1:1)*. His theme is 'eternal life' rather than 'the Kingdom'. His Jesus speaks in great discourses which are usually uttered after the performance of a miracle. There are only **seven 'signs'** or miracles in John but also there are **seven major 'I AM'** statements in which the Lord declares that he is the bread of life; the light

of the world; the Good Shepherd; the resurrection and the life; the way, the truth and the life; the Vine. Also, of course, in this gospel, there is the theme of the coming of the Spirit of truth – the Advocate or Counsellor.
(e) The gospel design: All the gospels, of course, are literary compositions. John's seems to be divided into two clear parts. First, the ministry of Jesus or *The Book of Signs (1:9 – 12:50)*. Second, the supper, farewell discourses, the passion and the resurrection *(13:1 – 20:31)*.
(f) John's titles for Jesus demonstrate his conviction about him. Jesus is the Saviour of the world; the Christ; the Word, the Lord, the King of Israel, the Son of God, the Son of Man. He also uses vivid expressions to describe discipleship: 'come, follow, enter, believe, dwell'. 'If you heed my commands, you will dwell in my love, as I have heeded my Father's commands and dwell in his love' *(15:10)*. Discipleship leads to eternal life.

8. The relationship of the fourth gospel with the synoptics
As one may expect, scholarly opinion differs on this as on other topics. Did John know and use the synoptics or did he not? Did he have his own quite independent Palestinian and/or other sources? For my part, I feel quite clear that whether John knew the written gospel of Mark or not, he certainly knew the synoptic tradition. In my view the key to understanding the fourth gospel is to realise that a great deal of what is **implicit in the Synoptics is made explicit in John**. If we place *Mark* at an early date, then it is possible John knew it and his gospel was intended to supplement and comment upon it as well as enabling his readers to share in his own deep penetration of the gospel story, the meaning of which is not knowledge or wisdom in any conventional sense, but love. 'I give you a new commandment: love one another; as I have loved you, so are you to love one another. If there is this love among you, then everyone will know that you are my disciples' *(13:34)*. 'I have spoken thus to you, so that my joy may be in you, and your joy complete. This is my commandment: love one another as I have loved you *(15:11,12)*.
Examples of John's explicitness are as follows:
(a) The theme of 'eternal life' is of more universal application than the 'coming of the kingdom'. John's meditation on what Jesus meant by kingdom – the reign or rule of love in a person's life – led him to emphasise the consequences of that reign for to dwell in Love, is to dwell in eternity here and now, whatever the life beyond death may bring.
(b) In *Mark (2:18–20)* Jesus drew a sharp distinction between the old forms of Judaism and the new life which his teaching brought. He likened the latter to new wine which burst out of the old skins. In *John (2:1–11)* we are actually presented with a situation in which Jesus turned water (the inadequate and insufficient Judaism) into wine which was abundant and

94

overflowing, more than anyone at the wedding could consume. This symbolised the new life which had come through Jesus. It is impossible to know what actually happened at this wedding celebration, but I cannot believe that Jesus turned water into wine, rather that his very presence there was in fact the 'new wine' and somehow saved the host from some kind of embarrassing situation. Thus, in John's gospel a sign can be interpreted as an acted parable or an act of symbolic truth. In the synoptics, the miracles were seen as manifestations of the kingdom of God. In *John* they are acts which show forth the glory of God in Jesus and hence his own glory.

(c) In Mark's gospel, Jesus raises Jairus' daughter. He says the child is not dead but sleeping *(5:39)*. In Luke's gospel, Jesus raises a widow's son, when the corpse of the young man is being carried out from the town of Nain on a bier. Luke makes it quite clear that he believed the widow's son to be dead. In John's gospel, Lazarus has been three days dead in his tomb before he is raised, but the whole point of the story is not the miracle but the conversation between Jesus and Martha, the sister of Lazarus. 'Jesus said, "Your brother will rise again". "I know that he will rise again", said Martha, "at the resurrection on the last day." Jesus said "I am the resurrection and the life. Whoever has faith in me shall live, even though he dies; and no one who lives and has faith in me shall die. Do you believe this?" "I do, Lord," she answered; "I believe that you are the Messiah, the Son of God, who was to come into the world"' *(11:23–25)*.

(d) Other **'I am'** statements

In Mark's gospel, we read of the feeding of the 5,000 and then much later of Jesus's words about the bread and and the wine at the Last Supper being his body and blood, i.e. the complete offering of himself to bring about a new relationship between humanity and God. In *John*, the feeding of the 5,000 results in the crowd wanting to make Jesus king but he evades them and goes up into the hills *(6:1–15)*. He later crosses the lake to Capernaum where he is again approached by many people and talks to them about 'the food of eternal life'. In the end he thoroughly alienates not only the Pharisees, but also some of his followers by saying, 'I am the bread of life. Whoever comes to me will never be hungry, and whoever believes in me will never be thirsty' *(6:35)*. John does not mention and therefore does not institutionalise Jesus' words at the last supper. He has something else to teach which refers to two other passages in the synoptics. In *Mark*, Jesus is very saddened by James' and John's request for pre-eminence and says 'the Son of Man did not come to be served but to serve' *(10:45)*. In *Luke*, the disciples' dispute as to which was the greatest, is placed at the last supper – 'Yet I am among you like a servant' *(22:24–27)*. However in *John*, the central action at the last supper is Jesus' actual washing of the disciples' feet

95

'I have set you an example: you are to do as I have done for you' (*John 13:15*).

In *Luke 11:33ff*, Jesus says, 'No one lights a lamp and puts it in a cellar, but on the lampstand so that those who come in may see the light'. And in *Matthew*, the saying is to the disciples, 'Like the lamp, you must shed light among your fellows' (*5:14–16*). In *John*, Jesus says, 'I am the light of the world. No follower of mine shall walk in darkness; he shall have the light of life' (*8:12*).

In '*Q*', Jesus says ask, seek and knock and the door of the kingdom will be opened, but in *John*, Jesus says 'I am the door; anyone who comes into the fold through me will be safe. He will go in and out and find pasture. A thief comes only to steal, kill and destroy; I have come that they may have life, and may have it in all its fullness' (*10:9,10*).

In '*Q*' we have the parable of the lost sheep, but in *John*, Jesus says, 'I am the good shepherd; the good shepherd lays down his life for his sheep. . . . But there are other sheep of mine, not belonging to this fold; I must lead them as well, and they too will listen to my voice' (*10:11,14,16*).

In *Mark*, Jesus says in effect that he has come to cure the sickness of sin, and to give his life as a ransom for many. In *John*, Jesus says 'I am the way, the truth, and the life' (*14:6*). The exclusiveness of the next words 'no one comes to the Father, except by me', should not, of course, be taken literally. If God is Love, then the way to God is by following the path of love, compassion, truth which is pre-eminently, but not exclusively, the way of Jesus. The Buddha also advocated the way of compassion.

In *Mark*, the parable of the sower describes the seed as the word of God. In *John*, the word is Jesus himself (*11:23–27*). In the synoptic parables the kingdom is likened to the mustard seed, and natural growth is used as a religious or spiritual metaphor. But in *John*, it is Jesus himself who is the vine. 'I am the vine, you are the branches. Anyone who dwells in me, as I dwell in him, bears much fruit' (*15:5*).

According to '*Q*', Jesus at the time of temptations refused any other role but that of the servant of the Lord. In *John*, Jesus says, 'The Son can do nothing by himself; he does only what he sees the Father doing' (*5:19*). 'As the Father has life in himself, so by his gift the Son also has life in himself (*5:26*).

(e) The **seven signs**

The first sign is a comprehensive introduction to the others. 'So Jesus performed in Cana-in-Galilee the first of the signs which revealed his glory and led his disciples to believe in him' (*2:11*). Then a Gentile sick boy is healed (*4:43–54*), a lame man walks and the healing takes place on the Sabbath! (*5:1–15*); the hungry are fed (*6:1–15*); a blind man receives his sight *(9:1–41)*; and a dead man is raised *(11:17–44)*. Some commentators would include walking on the water *(6:16–27)* which makes the raising of Lazarus the seventh sign. But many others would say that John's Greek word translated 'on' should really be rendered 'by'. So that Jesus was actually walking by the sea but on the shore. This means that the seventh sign is Jesus's own death and resurrection. These signs are reminiscent of Jesus' words to the disciples of John Baptist, when they come to ask whether Jesus really was the Messiah *(Luke 7:22)*; 'Go and tell John what you have seen and heard: the blind regain their sight, the lame walk, lepers are made clean, the deaf hear, the dead are raised to life, the poor are brought good news – and happy is he who does not find me an obstacle to faith'. John is not interested in signs merely as miracles or wonders but as symbolic of the life and purpose of Jesus himself.

A study of these comparisons illustrates that the teaching of Jesus in John, therefore, can be seen not as something very different from what is given in the synoptics, but as a concentration on and illumination of certain aspects of what was already there in the earlier tradition.

Further points

Women play a comparatively prominent part in John's gospel. Jesus' conversation with and attitude towards the Samaritan woman caused his disciples considerable astonishment. Mary, the mother of Jesus, appears at the beginning of the story at the wedding in Cana and is present at the foot of the cross. Martha makes a profound declaration of faith, equal to Peter's at Caesarea Philippi. Her sister, Mary, is also prominent in the story of Lazarus' raising.
Six days later, Jesus goes to have supper with Lazarus and his sisters. Mary anoints Jesus' feet with precious oil of nard, and wipes them with her hair *(12:1–3)*. And in the resurrection account, the risen Jesus appears first to Mary of Magdala, who had also been at the foot of the cross with Jesus' mother and her sister, Mary wife of Clopas.

The role of the Holy Spirit The Apostle John had been very close to the human Jesus during his earthly ministry. During the long years between the resurrection encounters and the actual writing of the gospel, his own life and outlook must have been strengthened and enlightened by the active presence of the Spirit. It is, therefore, from the depth of a lifetime's experience that he recollects Jesus' teaching and promise of the gift of this inward dwelling guide and counsellor. When Jesus was with them, they always had him to turn to in all their difficulties, but he promised that when he physically left them, they would not be bereft and desolate for the Father would give them the Spirit of truth. But this gift was dependent on their own relationship with Jesus; i.e. their commitment to the way of Love itself. 'If you love me, you will obey my commands; and I will ask the Father, and he will give you another to be your advocate, who will be with you for ever – the Spirit of truth' *(14:15–17)*.

In a further reference *(14:25–27)*, Jesus says 'I have told you these things while I am still with you; but the advocate, the Holy Spirit whom the Father will send in my name, will teach you everything and remind you of all that I have said. Peace is my parting gift to you, my own peace, such as the world cannot give'. We are reminded of Luke's story *(24:27,32)* when on the third day after Jesus' death, two of his disciples were walking sorrowfully on the road to Emmaus and were joined by a stranger who 'explained to them in the whole of scripture the things that referred to himself'. Then, over the breaking of bread, 'they recognised him as the Master, but he disappeared from their sight. They said to each other, 'Were not our hearts on fire as he talked with us on the road?' In Luke's story, this experience was an extraordinary happening, confined to those two disciples, but for John, the coming of the Spirit will be a universal experience for all those who follow Jesus. Further the gift of Jesus' peace will enhance the disciples' lives. John sees that Jesus is using the usual word for greeting and farewell, 'Shalom' in Hebrew, Peace in English, in a unique sense, for Jesus has overcome the powers of evil and will conquer death.

The theme of the Spirit figures prominently in *John 16* where Jesus warns his disciples of the hostility they will have to endure from others, including people who believe that in persecuting the followers of Jesus, they are doing God's will. Such was Paul's case before his encounter with the risen Jesus on the Damascan road: 'I myself once thought it my duty to work actively against the name of Jesus of Nazareth; and I did so in Jerusalem' *(Acts 26:9)*. But Jesus forewarns the disciples of his going and stresses that only after his departure will they be able to receive the advocate, the spirit of truth. 'If I do not go, the advocate will not come, whereas if I go, I will send him to you' *(16:7)*. The Spirit has a twofold job to perform. He will not only help, sustain and inspire the disciples, but he will also 'prove the world wrong about sin, justice and judgement'. Thus confirming the words of Simeon in Luke's gospel *(2:34,35)*, when he held the baby Jesus in his arms. The old prophet declared then that the state of people's hearts would be shown by their rejection or acceptance of Jesus. In *John*, the Spirit does not speak on his own authority. He is not an independent source for he will 'take what is mine and make it known to you' *(16:13,14)*.

Jesus' words from the cross. In John's gospel the crucified Jesus speaks three times: (i) 'Seeing his mother, with the disciple whom he loved standing beside her, Jesus said to her, "Mother, there is your son"; and to the disciple, "There is your mother"; and from that moment the disciple took her into his home' *(19:26,27)*. This is a moving tribute to Jesus' care for his mother but it is all the more interesting when we recall that he had brothers to whom the responsibility of his mother would naturally fall. However at that time Jesus' family were not believers, although according to *Acts*, James later became so and played a prominent part in the early church. Again we are reminded of a passage in *Mark* which affirms the reality for Jesus of his spiritual family. 'Whoever does the will of God is my brother and sister and mother' *(3:34)*.

(ii) 'After this, Jesus, aware that all had now come to its appointed end, said in fulfilment of scipture, "I am thirsty"' *(19:28)*. It would be absurd, of course, to suppose that Jesus said these words in order to fulfil *Psalm 22:15*, 'My mouth is dry as a potsherd and my tongue sticks to my gums; I am laid low in the dust of death'; or *Psalm 69:21b*, 'and when I was thirsty they gave me vinegar to drink'. But obviously *Psalm 22* was in his mind during the agony on the cross, for in *Mark* the first phrase of that psalm is the one recorded utterance of Jesus. Jesus' own terrible sufferings were remarkably identical with those of the faithful servant in *Psalm 22*; on the other hand, the desire for retribution on his enemies expressed in *Psalm 69*, is quite uncharacteristic of Jesus. Both psalms, however, end on a note of praise and hope. We can appreciate how essential it was for the first followers of Jesus, using their hindsight, to search for scriptural passages which fitted into the pattern of his life and death, even if that particular form of exegesis has relatively little value for us as modern readers.

(iii) Jesus was given a sponge soaked in sour wine. 'Having received the wine, he said, "It is accomplished!" Then he bowed his head and gave up his spirit' *(19:28,30)*. Mark records that 'Jesus gave a loud cry and died' *(Mark 15:37)* but it is John who reports that the cry was one of triumph. The task which Jesus had undertaken had been completed. In *Luke*, after the loud cry (perhaps as Jesus bent his head), he said 'Father, into your hands I commit my spirit' *(Luke 23:46)*.

We need to look carefully at the shift of emphasis in *John* for he focusses our attention away from the physical agony to the fact that the suffering was undertaken in the cause of love and that it brought its own vindication. This is the key to the whole Jesus story. Love is justified as the way of life, truth and spiritual growth. Jesus, according to John, knew this at the moment of death, not as the outcome of the resurrection, although this later event confirmed his faith. What is extraordinary is that at the point of death, Jesus gave a shout of triumph, not that his agony was over, but that he had done it – he had accomplished his task. This confirms and clarifies an earlier statement during Jesus' conversation with Nicodemus. 'Just as Moses lifted up the serpent in the wilderness, so the Son of Man must be lifted up, in order that everyone who has faith may in him have eternal life' *(3:14,15)*. According to the Moses' story in *Numbers 21:4–9*, the plague of fiery serpents was overcome by people looking up at the bronze serpent which Moses had made. This seems hardly credible to us, but we can appreciate the power which comes from faith in dynamic leadership. It was used by John to symbolise the triumph of Jesus **on** the cross when by his fidelity and love he overcame the powers of evil (portrayed in New Testament thought by the serpent, *cf. Revelation 12:9; 20:2)* and eventually death.

Jesus showed, that vicarious suffering, undeserved but undertaken in the cause of love, is a most powerful instrument with unimaginable effects. Its potency arises from the creative urge within the universe itself. This is the witness of John to the efficacy of Jesus' crucifixion and why he makes the claim that Jesus is the Saviour of the World.

Conclusion

The greatness of his gospel lies in the fact that John is superbly expressing the truth of lived experience. This experiential truth is of a different category from the verifiable statements which our culture is accustomed to see as the only truth but it is nevertheless completely valid in its own sphere for the individual concerned. For example, a factual assessment of the different order of events in *John* and *Mark* would lead us to ask the question – did Jesus cleanse the temple at the beginning or end of his ministry? Personally I think Mark is correct in placing it at the end, for it was the culminating event which caused the whole Sanhedrin to think they must dispose of Jesus as quickly as possible. However, I can appreciate that for John the symbolic meaning of Jesus' action was of far greater importance than precise timing. In *John* it is the conversation which follows the cleansing which gives the clue to its meaning. 'The Jews challenged Jesus: "What sign can you show to justify your action?" "Destroy this temple," Jesus replied, "and in three days, I will raise it up again".' For the Jews, of course, this was nonsense but John explains for his readers: 'But the temple he was speaking of was his body. After his resurrection his disciples recalled what he had said' *(2:12–22)*.

Again, I do not personally think that Jesus had the power to raise someone from the dead, although I have no doubt that he had quite extraordinary healing gifts. The symbolism, or the sign of the raising of

Lazarus is that it prefigures Jesus' own resurrection in the three days of the gospel story. To credit him with 'raising the dead' seems to me at best an irrelevance and at worst a diminishing of the humanity which is the most challenging aspect of the Jesus we meet in Mark's gospel. However, I can say with Martha, that I do believe 'Jesus is the resurrection and the life' in the profoundest and deepest sense of those words. If this is my experience and the experience of countless others down the centuries, how much more so was it the experiential truth known by John, the beloved disciple.

As a young man, John was not only one of Jesus' first disciples but also one of his closest friends. He was with Jesus throughout his ministry and at his death. He ran to the empty tomb with Peter on that momentous first day of the week. The resurrection experience of Jesus came to him and to the others and completely changed their lives. He was prominent in the early part of Luke's second volume, the *Acts of the Apostles*, when the disciples received the gift of the Spirit and later when he appeared with Peter before the Sanhedrin (*Acts 4:20*). According to tradition, he eventually went to live in Ephesus and died there before the end of the century. His profound meditation and interpretation of his master grew from years of discipleship and apostleship. He himself implied that the Spirit of truth, active in his life, was his inspiration in writing.

CHAPTER FOURTEEN

A note on Paul's view of Jesus

1. THERE IS NO EVIDENCE either from *Acts* or from his letters, that Paul knew Jesus in the flesh. He was present at Stephen's death, however, and was obviously deeply affected by it. The manner of Stephen's dying was probably the catalyst which prepared him for his encounter with the risen Jesus on the Damascan Road. Paul was, however, a close colleague of those men who had known the historic Jesus: Simon Peter and James, Jesus' brother. Further he says emphatically in *1 Cor. 15:3* that he handed on the facts which had been imparted to him by the leaders of the Christian community. His first recorded sermon in *Acts 13* follows closely on those by Peter, except for a hint of justification by faith which was to become a keynote in Paul's theology *(v.39)*. When we study his letters in detail we discover that he knew well the attested facts of Jesus' life and teaching.

2. Nevertheless Paul's own personal experience and witness was to **Jesus the risen Christ**. His favourite title for Christ is 'Lord' or 'Our Lord' which would have an exalted meaning for Gentiles. But he was not the first to use this term. 'Jesus is Lord' was probably the earliest Christian confession of faith *(c.f Romans 10:9* and *1 Cor. 12:3)*. The aim of all Paul's work was to bring others into this relationship: 'It is not ourselves that we proclaim; we proclaim Christ Jesus as Lord, and ourselves as your servants for Jesus' sake' *(1 Cor. 4:5)*. Paul also calls Jesus 'Son of God'. 'My present mortal life is lived by faith in the Son of God who loved me and gave himself up for me' *(Gal. 2:20)*. Other titles include The Wisdom of God *(1 Cor. 1:24)*, The Lord of Glory *(1 Cor. 2:8)* and The Last Adam *(1 Cor. 15:45ff)*.

3. It is often said (cf. Karen Armstrong's *The first Christian: Paul's impact on Christianity*) that Christianity in its orthodox form relies more on Paul than on Jesus. If this is so (and I am not convinced it is true) then it is not Paul's fault. He was true to his experience and his continuing relationship with the risen Lord and he interpreted this according to his rich background

and fine mind. Succeeding generations may have taken his letters as the literal Word of God and therefore regarded them as sacrosanct, but his contemporaries did not necessarily so consider them. We know he had bitter enemies. But his friends and converts realised his worth and regarded his written word as authoritative hence most of his letters have been preserved.

Paul's letters were written to converts who already knew the main facts about the historical Jesus, so he does not waste time in dealing with the same kind of material as the gospels. Apart from *Romans*, his epistles were written in the heat of the moment to meet specific needs in the churches which he had founded. His approach in *Romans* is different because he had not established the Roman church, although he had many friends there. The latter is a profound statement of his faith and has been fittingly called his gospel.

I admire Paul deeply without necessarily agreeing with him. Seeing him in his cultural context, I cannot help appreciating the amazing change which Jesus the Christ brought about in his life. He did become a new man, but still a man of his time, for all his immense vision. Inevitably some aspects of his theology reflect very much a 1st-century view. It was when these aspects became fixed in orthodoxy by later readers that they gave rise to a static faith.

4. It is not possible to deal adequately with Paul's theology in a few pages but a brief look at **Galatians** will illustrate some of the above points. *Galatians* may well have been the first letter that he wrote about AD 49, when on his way to what Luke *(Acts 15)*, describes as the 'Council of Jerusalem'. It is a very personal, controversial letter, written in such white hot passion that sometimes his sentences are not properly constructed. It gives us a complete picture of the man and his theology. For this reason many scholars date *Galatians* during Paul's time at Ephesus in AD 57, but I prefer the earlier date.

(a) Paul had founded four churches in Galatia (Pisidian Antioch, Iconium, Lystra and Derbe). When he went back to Syrian Antioch, he heard that trouble had arisen in these four Christian communities on the crucial issue of entry into the church. The letter makes it clear that certain Judaistic Christians (called Judaizers) had gone to Galatia after Paul had left, disturbing the new Gentile converts not only with their views on circumcision but by a personal attack on Paul in which they challenged the truth of his gospel and his right to preach it. These devout Jewish Christians believed that Gentiles should first become Jews (through the rite of circumcision which symbolised an acceptance of the whole Jewish Law) before they could be baptised into the new faith in Christ. Paul and

Barnabas realised that this was completely unacceptable. Paul knew from his personal experience that the Law could not bring anyone into a right relationship with God. The purpose of the Law was to show up inadequacy and failure. Paul says, 'if righteousness comes by law, then Christ died for nothing' *(2:21)*.

(b) The issue was crucial if the religion of Jesus was to be liberated from Judaism. In *Mark 2*, Jesus himself is recorded as having told two short parables about the old and the new where he likens his own teaching to the new wine which would of necessity burst out of the old rigid wineskin. Jesus introduced an entirely new principle which made the Law, as such, superfluous. His was an inward religion of the pure heart and the redirected will. To Paul, therefore, the Law was temporary and provisional. He likened it to a teacher or guardian. It had its place in the childhood of humanity but now it had been superseded by Grace. The only condition of entry into the church was faith, faith in the Lord Jesus Christ. This was Paul's own experience which had released him from the bondage of sin and the Law. In fact Paul delivered the young and growing Christian church from the restrictions of the Jewish Law. It is ironic that a whole structure of legalistic Christianity built upon his thought, has restrained millions of believers down the centuries to this day.

(c) Paul saw humanity as tainted by the fall of Adam, whom he believed in as an actual historical person. He had tried to find his way back to God through being a devout Pharisee. He tells us in *Philippians* how scrupulous he had been in keeping the Law, but he needed the transforming power of Jesus Christ to set him free and put him into a right relationship with God. For him, it was the cross of Christ which made all this possible. Yet Jesus had become accursed under the Law by accepting death through crucifixion. If this could happen to the Son of God then the Law's falliblity was clearly demonstrated.

We may not agree with Paul's analysis of the human condition, but surely we can sympathise and identify with his former sense of futility and frustration. We have potentiality for good and evil and above all else we are very easily moulded and influenced. But the great spirits amongst us have broken free, understanding their own motivation and originating fresh ideas. Paul experienced a profound change of direction through his encounter with Jesus. He felt himself to be under a new law, the law of love and he began his new life with the sense of belonging to love, and to Christ *(5:14, 6:2)*.

The symbol and reality of the cross has been distorted down the centuries, but it is basically the symbol of love – a love that would not give up, that endured to the end. It is love that liberates, empowers, transforms. We know this from our own experience for when we love deeply we are capable of achieving the impossible, our best efforts are transcended and we go beyond our known capacity.

(d) Paul believed that this present world lay under the power of evil. He thought there were mysterious forces which ruled the universe and which inspired awe and worship in pagan humanity. Humanity was enslaved to sin and separated from God. But all this was to change for a new age had dawned with the coming of Jesus Christ. He felt himself to be living in the last stages of the old order and the dawn of the new. Very soon Jesus Christ would return with glory and establish his kingdom. In some respects, therefore, his is an interim ethic before the new era begins. For example, he did not extol virginity and celibacy for their own sake but because he felt it was out of place to beget children when the end of the world was imminent. He was wrong about this, of course, as perhaps Jesus himself was, in anticipating the end of all things. All we know for certain about Jesus' view of the end of the world, was that he said 'Yet about that day or hour no one knows, not even the angels in heaven, not even the Son; no one but the Father' *(Mark 13:32)*. Jesus, however, did correctly foresee the terrible crisis that later came upon his own people.
On the other hand, in one sense Paul was right: the coming of Jesus brought a totally new dimension into human affairs.

(e) *Galatians 3:1 – 4:31* is known as the doctrinal argument for the truth of the gospel as Paul understood it. Freedom and new life come through faith in the Lord Jesus Christ. This cannot be enhanced in any way by rigid adherence to the Jewish law (as his detractors had emphasised). His appeal to the experience of the Galatians themselves shows how successful he had been in his missionary work. 'When God gives you the Spirit and works miracles among you, is it because you keep the law, or is it because you have faith in the gospel message?' *(3:5)*. Many of the succeeding passages show clearly Paul's rabbinical training. His allegory of Sarah and Hagar *(4:21–31)* strikes very little response in us; and although his use of texts from the Abraham stories was obviously very effective in countering the claims of the Judaizers, these texts cannot have the same significance for us. Yet the letter as a whole contains some marvellous and illuminating ideas, way ahead of their time.

'It is through faith that you are all Sons of God in union with Christ Jesus. Baptised into union with him, you have all put on Christ as a garment. There is no such thing as Jew and Greek, slave and freeman, male and female; for you are all one person in Christ Jesus' (3:26–28).

Paul attached great importance to baptism for it was at this rite that the believer professed his faith in Jesus Christ. This was the formal admission into the community of Christ and was sufficient in itself. The beautiful metaphor of 'putting on Christ as a garment' reached back to the Old Testament idea of being 'clothed in righteousness'. In some subtle way, the wearer became identified with what had been put on. So at the conclusion of the letter Paul can say 'Circumcision is nothing; uncircumcision is nothing; the only thing that counts is new creation' (6:15). And in this new creation, the superiority, even contempt which the Jew felt, not only for Gentiles, but also for women and slaves, would simply not exist. Paul's vision, therefore, was of a future community in which racial, gender, social or class divisions no longer operated because Jesus' way, the way of respect and compassion, was paramount. This can be a global ideal in which we are all involved and for which we can all work, whether we actually acknowledge the lordship of Jesus or not.

'To prove that you are sons, God has sent into our hearts the Spirit of his Son, crying "Abba! Father!" You are therefore no longer a slave but a son' (4:6f). Paul saw humanity as a spiritual child who had yet to reach maturity and freedom. Both Jew and Gentile were in bondage, but through the activity of the Spirit, humanity's final destiny was to become in fact the son/daughter of God with all the fullness of life that this involved. We may not express our 'bondage' in Pauline terms but we need to understand and therefore be free of the complexities which cripple and deny our full personal affirmation. 'It is for freedom that Christ set us free. Stand firm, therefore, and refuse to submit again to the yoke of slavery' (5:1).

'The only thing that counts is faith expressing itself through love' (5:6). Here is the heart of Paul's message: the interrelation of faith in the Lord Jesus Christ, which works out in the loving lives of his believers. 'Serve one another in love. For the whole law is summed up in a single commandment: "Love your neighbour as yourself" ' (5:14).
(Paul's finest description of love's qualities is to be found in *1 Corinthians 13*, and probably what he is actually giving us is a pen picture of Jesus.)

'But the harvest of the Spirit is love, joy, peace, patience, kindness, goodness, fidelity, gentleness and self-control. Against such things there is no law. Those who belong to Christ Jesus have crucified the old nature with its passions and desires. If the Spirit is the source of our life, let the Spirit also direct its course' (5:22–25).
Lists of vices and virtues occur in Paul's letters. Vices are not simply an offence against society but against God. They are the product of a wrong orientation which Paul calls 'the old or lower nature'. The only way to deal with them is not by suppression or regulation but by 'crucifixion'. We need

to interpret this in modern terms bearing in mind that the cross is the symbol of fidelity and love. It is love which enables us to face the inner motivation which prompted the wrong action, and bring it out into the open. It is love which desires change and gives the courage and faith to pursue a different course. The church tended to think that the Spirit manifested itself through extraordinary signs such as prophecy or 'speaking with tongues' but Paul saw that when the Spirit was an inward reality then an individual's life quite naturally showed forth love, joy and peace, the harvest of 'that of God within'.

For Paul the spirit of Christ was now the inner spring of his action. Through its activity the personality could develop into full freedom as a member of a worshipping community. He expressed this conviction in different terms in his first letter to the *Corinthians*; 'The first man, Adam, became a living creature, whereas the last Adam has become a life giving spirit' (*15:45*). This second Adam, therefore, has brought into being a new kind of humanity.

(e) Today Paul is blamed for some of the unpleasant excesses of the church: for unhealthy masochism, the denigration of women and of sexual love; a false emphasis on authority, etc. But it is the constant predilection of human minds to formalise and ossify the insights of genius. The history of the great religions shows this pattern repeated again and again. But we must ourselves break free under the inspiration of the Spirit or Inner Light and in our fellowship with one another.
William James said, 'Religion is not dogma but experience', and William Blake 'I see through the eye, not with it'.

CHAPTER FIFTEEN

The Jesus of the Gospels
and the Christ of faith

IT HAS NOT BEEN POSSIBLE, OF COURSE, to cover the whole of the New Testament, but through looking at the synoptics and *John* – however briefly – we have seen how the presentation of Jesus was changed by the startling perspective of the resurrection experience, the empowerment brought by the gift of the Spirit and the horizons opened up by missionary activity. It is not a profitable speculation to discuss here what may have happened on that third day after Jesus had died, but it is a fact of history that his first disciples, both men and women, experienced his presence amongst them in a totally convincing way. They knew that he had passed through death and was alive in the profoundest sense. We have confirmation of this experience not only from the writings of Luke, Matthew and John, but also from Paul's letter to the *Corinthians*, written about AD 55 –

'First and foremost, I handed on to you the tradition I had received: that Christ died for our sins, in accordance with the scriptures; that he was buried; that he was raised to life on the third day, in accordance with the scriptures; and that he appeared to Cephas (Peter), and afterwards to the Twelve. Then he appeared to over 500 of our brothers at once, most of whom are still alive, though some have died. Then he appeared to James (the brother of Jesus, who became leader of the Jerusalem church) and afterwards to all the apostles. Last of all he appeared to me too; it was like a sudden abnormal birth. For I am the least of the apostles, indeed not fit to be called an apostle, because I had persecuted the church' (*1 Cor. 15:3–11*).

Besides the written evidence of the New Testament documents practically all of which can be dated within the first century AD, we also have the emergence of the historic Christian church. This was founded by men and women who were utterly transformed by their experience of Jesus' resurrection and by their continuing awareness of his spirit working within them. They preached of Jesus' resurrection, which had confirmed for them that he was the Christ. 'Now Jesus has been raised by God, and of this we are all witnesses. Exalted at God's right hand he received from the Father, the promised Holy Spirit, and all that you now see and hear flows from him' (Peter's first sermon, after the gift of the Spirit as reported in *Acts 2 : 32,33*).

After the resurrection day, these original disciples, all of whom were Jews for whom the sabbath was sacred, began to keep also the first day of the week as the Lord's day *(Revelation 1:10)*. Eventually this day took precedence over the institution of the Jewish sabbath to become the holy day of the Christian church.

According to *Acts*, the risen Jesus 'showed himself (to the disciples) after his death and gave ample proof that he was alive: he was seen by them over a period of 40 days and spoke to them about the kingdom of God' *(Acts 1:3)*. Whatever took place at the Ascension, the experience made it clear to the disciples that they could no longer expect to see Jesus in person as they had done.

There are numerous difficulties for 20th-century readers in Luke's story of the Ascension, but they stem from the fact that we seek for literal rather than experiential truth. For first-century people, God was 'up there' in the heavens and the disciples pictured their exalted Lord as 'seated at God's right hand'. They had experienced the gift of the Spirit both personally and communally; its activity was further proof of the fulfilment of their Lord's ministry. It would be absurd to expect them to express all this in terms which were inappropriate to their particular culture and tradition. As 20th-century readers, we do not believe that God is sitting on a golden throne in what we now call outer space. Nor can we visualise Jesus ascending into the heavens and the appearance of two men robed in white who said 'Men of Galilee, why stand there looking up into the sky? This Jesus who has been taken from you up to heaven will come in the same way as you have seen him go' *(Acts 1:11)*. But we can and do experience the internalisation of relationships. When our loved ones die, their presence may seem to be quite clearly still with us for a short space of time, then the relationship changes as we endeavour to become accustomed to their physical absence. We still have a sense of communion but of a quite different kind, very hard to describe. What love creates, is never destroyed. Death can be the gateway into the world of Light.

Because of his relationship with the Father, Jesus was totally convinced of the reality of life after death. He was thus able to give his friends strong assurances that their relationship with him would continue. 'Set your troubled hearts at rest. Trust in God always; trust also in me. There are many dwelling-places in my Father's house; if it were not so I should have told you; for I am going to prepare a place for you. And if I go and prepare a place for you, I shall come again and take you to myself, so that where I am you may be also; and you know the way I am taking.' When Thomas answered that he did not know the way, Jesus declared, 'I am the way, the truth and the life' *(John 14:1–6)*. And Jesus' way is that of love.

According to Luke, Jesus also promised something similar to the crucified criminal hanging beside him, who begged to be remembered by Jesus, 'Truly I tell you: today you will be with me in Paradise' *(Luke 23:43)*.

Jesus' first disciples did not work out a doctrinal system for their faith. But from *Acts* and the *Letters*, a pattern emerges in their preaching and teaching. From Luke's account of Peter's four sermons in *Acts*, C. H. Dodd (*The Apostolic preaching and its developments*, Hodder & Stoughton, 1936) has listed six points: The last days have dawned; the death and resurrection of Jesus, shown to be in accord with Old Testament prophecy, have inaugurated the last days; Jesus is now exalted at God's right hand, as Lord and Christ; the Holy Spirit in the church is the sign of Christ's present power; Christ will shortly return in glory: all those who hear are called upon to repent and believe. We can appreciate how this Apostolic preaching came about, but it is not necessary for us to identify with it in every clause. Firstly, the Apostles were wrong in their timing for they expected their master to return in glory quite soon at the end of the world. Secondly, for them it was essential to see Jesus as the fulfilment of Old Testament prophecy so they searched their well known and loved scriptures to find possible texts. Jesus himself, as was perfectly natural, used his people's ancient writings to convey his ideas and thoughts, especially from the prophets. We may find it hard, however, to understand inwardly the preciousness of books in a culture where very few existed and the channels of communication were quite different from our own. Thirdly, the Jews of that era were a subject people, longing for freedom from the Roman yoke through armed rebellion or through God's direct intervention; they saw the anticipated coming of the Messiah as the culmination of God's dealing with Israel. Hence we find eschatological emphasis in the Apostles' preaching and the use of like-minded prophets, such as *Joel (2:31)*, *Zechariah (9:14)* and *Daniel*. Jesus was also declared to be of Davidic line and therefore the rightful inheritor of God's promise.

Jesus was indeed a Jew steeped in the faith of his ancestors and it would be shortsighted to attempt to divorce him from his cultural background. But for me, Jesus was primarily an innovator. Important though his Old Testament background is, his significance is not a matter of fulfilling Old Testament scriptures. When we see his context clearly, however, his radical outlook and emphasis on forgiveness appears all the more remarkable.

There were those amongst the first or second generation believers in Jesus who wished to contain their new faith within the boundaries of Judaism. Matthew's concept of the ideal disciple as a rabbi who also understood the kingdom as Jesus taught it, was limited. In his gospel he reports Jesus as saying 'I did not come to abolish, but to complete. Truly I tell you: so long as heaven and earth endure not a letter, not a dot, will disappear from the law until all that must happen has happened' *(Matthew 5:17-20)*. It is clear from Jesus' life that if he ever spoke these words, he must have done so with characteristic irony.

In the letter to the *Hebrews* (author unknown), we find the same approach, with the new faith being constrained within the limitations of Judaic Christianity. But the behaviour of the free spirits of Peter, Stephen, Paul and Barnabas, as reported in *Acts* and the *Letters*, shows how the early church struggled to free itself from the confinement of Judaism so that baptism 'in the name of the Father and the Son and the Holy Spirit' *(Matthew 28:19)* became the rite of entry into the church. It was not preceded by circumcision and Jewish food laws were eventually abandoned. The centre of Jewish Christianity lay in Jerusalem but after the city's fall in AD 70 and subsequent desolation for many years, Jewish Christianity eventually died out.

Jesus' first disciples did not work out a theology of redemption as such. They taught from their own experience and consequently its implications for others. They were drawn to Jesus by his compassionate understanding. His love reached out and helped them to see deeply within themselves; to long to be different people, to receive forgiveness for all their failures, to set their faces in another direction, to be made new. They emerged empowered from this total encounter and, despite setbacks, they walked in his company for the rest of their lives.

So in *1 Peter* we read a passage which speaks poignantly of Jesus' sufferings: 'He carried our sins in his own person on the gibbet, so that we might cease to live for sin and begin to live for righteousness. By his wounds you have been healed *(1 Peter 2:24,25)*. Later comes the phrase 'Christ too suffered for our sins once and for all, the just for the unjust, that he might bring us to God' *(3:18)*. The 'once and for all' has become part of credal Christianity. But its experiential meaning can be lost under stated formula. Jesus' act of sacrificial love has unique significance because he was the innovator, the one who set in motion a whole chain of events. And because his act of love was vindicated by the resurrection experience of those who loved him, they in turn received his power and discovered it to be ever present in their daily lives. In this sense Jesus' life and person was unique but what he was and did had universal application.

111

The New Testament documents are records of a living encounter with the Jesus of Nazareth who became Jesus the Christ. It was later that a formulated creed emerged which became the doctrine of the church which bears his title, a nickname given at Antioch *(Acts 11:26)* by the pagan population to explain the extraordinary spectacle of both Jews and Gentiles meeting together in worship!

In the early days of the first century, the credal affirmation of converts, would appear to be simply the declaration that 'Jesus is Lord'. But for the next five centuries at least, the church endeavoured to work out its faith in its living Lord. Of particular concern was the relationship between Christ, the Holy Spirit and God, given the strong Hebraic conviction that God is one, also the whole question of the divinity and humanity of Jesus the Christ. Amongst bitter controversy and accusations of deviation and heresy, several important Councils met and attempted to resolve these matters. Amongst the most influential was that called by the Emperor Constantine at Nicaea (AD 325) to settle the dispute caused by the Arian heresy. (Arius believed the Son could not be identified with the Godhead. He was only God in a derivative sense.) This was known as the first great Ecumenical Council and from its formula came what is now known as the Nicene Creed. This creed focuses on Christ's eternal pre-existence and glorious after-life. It says nothing about his early career except that he was born and died.

In some respects the Christ of the church became a different concept from the Jesus of the gospel. Christ the Pantocrator seems a product more of the hierarchical structure of the Byzantine Church rather than a faithful rendering of the gospel Jesus. And Christ as the second person of the Trinity seemed so removed from the human situation that Mary, mother of the Jesus of the gospels, was elevated to act as intercessor on behalf of repentant sinners. In Roman Catholicism we find the doctrines not only of the Immaculate Conception of Mary (that she was herself conceived without the taint of original sin) but also the Assumption, which states that she was carried directly up to heaven at the time of her death. These beliefs, however hallowed by tradition and use, are not substantiated by New Testament studies.

Outstanding Christian religious dissidents, such as Martin Luther and George Fox, have sought for renewal of faith by going back to the New Testament (and the scriptures generally) to rediscover for their time and age the truths embodied there. In George Fox's case, particularly, it was experiential truth that he sought, 'What canst thou say?' And he expressed this lived experience, not in a doctrine or a formulated creed, but as truth seen in terms of his own time. I believe we have to do the same today.

Long before I knew anything much of George Fox, in my teaching of religious and biblical studies, I was endeavouring to discover inner truth and the different planes of interpretation of this truth as revealed in the lives, thoughts and writings of ancient peoples. I was seeking also to discuss these matters in terms that were comprehensible to 20th-century youngsters. This was how the Jesus of the gospel became central to my own faith. I believe that through the resurrection, the human Jesus was translated into the Christ, releasing the spiritual power of Love which enables the believer to be energised and motivated anew.

I find myself unable to say the Nicene creed. I understand the historical circumstances which led to the emphasis on Christ's eternal pre-existence and after-life but I cannot agree with the interpretation which was then put upon the Prologue to John's gospel: 'In the beginning the Word already was. The Word was in God's presence, and what God was, the Word was. He was with God at the beginning, and through him all things came to be; without him no created thing came into being' *(1:1–3)*.

Precursors of these ideas are found in the Wisdom Literature of the Old Testament, where the personalised female figure of Wisdom (Greek: Sophia) was thought of as the companion and helper of God in the creation of the world *(Proverbs 8, Ecclesiasticus 24,* and *Wisdom 7:22 – 8:1)* and as the inspirer of right conduct in people's lives. But John does not use the Greek 'sophia', rather 'logos' which his readers could have identified with the 'Logos' of Greek Stoic thought, or with the creative word spoken by God to bring the universe into being: 'God said "let there be light"' *(Genesis 1:3)*.

So human minds have struggled to express ideas of divine immanence and we must continue the effort, for the specific incarnation of the 'Word' or 'Logos' in the person of Jesus raises all kinds of problems. If we believe that there is that of God within each human being, or that in biblical terms humanity was made in God's image and received the divine breath, i.e. the spirit, then each of us is also incarnate. But when does this happen? At what point between the moment of conception and the moment of birth is a human being created? Christians find themselves unable to agree. Personally I incline to believe with Wordsworth that 'that of God within us' is preincarnate and 'trailing clouds of glory do we come From God, who is our home'. We are all potentially God's children but need to develop and encourage the growth of the spirit to inherit our full destiny. We are all unique, but Jesus realised the latent potential in a human being to become the Son of God in a very special sense, indeed the Christ.

For many today, the concept of Christ stands for the archetypal spirit, dwelling within human beings before any historical manifestation. This spirit may or may not be equated with the Jesus of the gospels, or the Inner

113

Light. The great religious of all ages and faiths have experienced its indwelling, its power and energy, regardless of the name by which it has been known to them.

The relationship between the gospel Jesus and the Christ of faith is something which has to be worked out by each concerned individual to whom the Christian tradition is important. In this intense study we always encounter profound mystery. Although I believe our rational selves must be engaged in the exercise to try to translate into words what we know in another dimension of our being, there are some things which cannot be explained or even understood, except on a level that has more to do with intuition and experiential awareness than logic. It is in the wonder of genuine worship, whatever form it may take, that we can touch upon this inner reality and find communion with each other regardless of intellectual difficulties.

CHAPTER SIXTEEN

The relevance of Jesus
to some contemporary issues

IN MY INTRODUCTION, I SUGGESTED THAT JESUS had something essential to contribute to the solving of our human dilemmas. In the succeeding chapters we have looked at the Jesus of the gospels and tried to discern the experiential truth there expressed. We have also briefly seen how the human Jesus became translated into the Christ, to become the centre of faith for millions of people. But what of his contemporary relevance? Jesus claimed, in effect, to have come to cure the sickness of sin (*Mark 2:13–17*) which for him and his contemporary Jewish culture meant the word or action which contravened the law of God. But Jesus also summarised this ancient law in terms of love: wholehearted love of God and love of neighbour as oneself. He also gave his disciples a golden rule: to treat others as they would like to be treated themselves. We can say, therefore, that it was the unloving thought, word and action which, for Jesus, constituted sin.

Jesus' own life and teaching show us possibly three or more aspects to this cure of sin.
(i) We must understand our own motivation. Whereas the Mosaic law forbade murder, Jesus forbade the hatred and anger which, if not dealt with, could lead to murderous thoughts. These were in themselves self-destroying, but they could also lead to fatal actions against others (*Matthew 5:21–22*).
(ii) Jesus made the outrageous demand that we have to be willing to forgive and to be forgiven (*Mark 11:25*), only so can the power of compassionate love be released. We long to achieve harmony within ourselves and with each other but we fail, hence our sense of guilt. The biblical narrative emphasises the fact of broken relationships; between God and humanity, between men, women and children, between humanity and the animal kingdom. What the bible offers, on its own terms, is reconciliation at every

level. But it is Jesus who introduces the new factor of forgiveness into human activities. When we do wrong, we must seek forgiveness of God, of each other and ourselves. This is not done by rite, ritual, or propitiatory sacrifice, but within. Things have to be put right as far as they can be and the psychological, emotional and physical damage worked through and healed. This is a quite different process from the enforcement of the civil law of a country, which if broken, ensures that penalties are forthcoming both as a deterrent to further law breaking and as a punishment for that particular infringement.

The history of humanity clearly shows that retaliation only makes matters worse. But is forgiveness weakness? How is forgiveness possible when we suffer and those whom we love suffer terrible things, such as torture, injustice, concentration camps, oppression and death? Jesus himself was not at all weak. He had immense strength and he did not hestitate to speak out against hypocrisy and exploitation. He could not be silenced except by torture and death. Yet he also forgave the soldiers as they nailed him to the cross. Even in his agony he was able to get inside another person's skin realising that the soldiers did not understand what they were doing, they were simply obeying orders. He even found the strength to think for his mother, his friend and the dying thief beside him. The crucifixion itself can be tragically misread if it is seen as the destruction of Jesus and all his hopes. Because he was not deflected by all that happened to him, death was the means of rebirth. Hatred, revenge, bitterness, unresolved conflict, uncontrolled or unchannelled anger, even fear, are the truly destructive elements within the human soul. These Jesus fought and overcame. The message of the cross is that because Jesus held fast to love he was able to go through the experience of desolation and agony to reach that transformed state which lies beyond pain and death.

(iii) His secret lay in freedom from self-concern, although he clearly recognised that there was a proper place for self-love. He did not undervalue himself or his power over others, but he did not allow recognition of his own charisma to corrupt him. From the story of the temptations, we can deduce that he was also a prey to self-doubt at times and certainly he thought of alternative means of bringing in his concept of the kingdom of God. However he rejected them because he was convinced that true greatness was service to others, not being served. He knew that humanity had basic spiritual needs, because we are 'made in the image of God', and that evil means could not be used to achieve a noble end because in the process human beings become corrupted by the evil. Men and women can be easily influenced, persuaded or deceived by sham and falsity, so Jesus believed the only valid power was that of love which gives of itself for the sake of the

116

other. He knew that the ability to love even his enemies, came from God, who was Love. So he completely trusted in the way that Love led him, even to his death. He was uncorrupted. His fidelity was not shaken by the hatred of his enemies or the treachery of Judas (for whom he felt deep compassion), or even by the inability of his friends, especially Peter, to remain steadfast. But that was not the end of the story. The resurrection experience and the gift of the Holy Spirit brought his disciples renewed faith in him, so that they felt the same powerful freedom in their lives.

(iv) Jesus was a realist. He identified the underlying weakness in the human personality and therefore the need of self-understanding and a transforming power. He felt this need could be answered when the indwelling reign of God, of Love, was established in a person's life. He himself lived out his beliefs, hence his personal power and influence.

I know that believers have worshipped Jesus as God for nearly 2,000 years, but I think this tells us more about human beings than about Jesus. In deifying him we have robbed Jesus of his pre-eminent right to speak with authority to the human condition. I see him as a quite extraordinary and unique person who by his very love and fidelity became the Christ. The text of the Old and New Testaments has been regarded as the untouchable word of God, to be totally accepted as authoritative and final. But by presenting Jesus as the living word of God, or the human face of the divine, the prologue to John's gospel gives us all a vision of our ultimate destiny as 'children of Light'. Potentially, we all belong to that ultimate reality of Love.

In the same way, Jesus' personal act of self-giving has become formalised into a rite or a creed and the power of his transforming experience has been treated almost as a magic formula capable of solving from the outside the deep seated problems of imbalance within the human psyche. But his teaching and life were directly personal; he drove people to look deep within themselves, at their understanding and inner motivation, so that they could change the direction of their lives, inspired by love and working in community with others.

What has all this to say to our present situation? I would guess that no other century has seen such enormous changes in outlook, lifestyles and population trends. I cannot attempt to gaze into the future or give a full picture of the contemporary scene, but certain central issues face humanity as it goes into the 21st century.

First: the Environment There has been considerable growth in awareness of the dangers which face us through pollution of our planet. We have only just begun to grasp the side-effects of our industrial processes as seen in the poisoned air, rivers and countryside which are creating great health hazards. We are learning more about the greenhouse effect and damage to the ozone layer. Many beautiful species are threatened with extinction. It is a vast subject. We inhabit a very different world from the one in which Jesus lived and we may ask how could he have anything to say about environmental matters. He did not, of course, mention them as such, but he was very clear indeed about greed and love of money, generally the motivation behind ruthless and selfish exploitation. He also talked of the right perspective in human life *(Matthew 6:24–30)*. If his words about taking no thought for the morrow, like birds of the air or the lilies of the field, are interpreted completely literally, how easy to dismiss them as unrealistic and naive idealism. But if they are taken as poetic, vivid pictures of a certain fundamental attitude of mind and approach to life itself, how challenging and potent they become. While we are unlikely to personalise the fecundity of nature or think of God as 'feeding' the birds or 'clothing' the grass, we should not misread Jesus' pictorial imagery. Elsewhere he contrasts the workings of nature with human beings: nature is not morally selective; '[the heavenly Father] causes the sun to rise on good and bad alike, and sends the rain on the innocent and the wicked' *(5:45)*. He sees in the natural world around him a divine creativity which ensures a stable natural order. How much more effective men and women can be, if they use their moral sense to choose of their own free will to cooperate with the energy and purpose of the divine love. Jesus was even more explicit when he said 'Do not store up for yourselves treasure on earth, where moth and rust destroy, and thieves break in and steal; but store up treasure in heaven, where neither moth nor rust will destroy, nor thieves break in and steal. For where your treasure is, there will your heart be also' *(Matthew 6:19–21)*. The literal high-minded reader might say that the purely motivated person should avoid laying up any kind of treasure. But Jesus knew that human beings do value and treasure what they consider to be most precious. He is saying – look again at that which you do value above all else: is it worthy of your trust and of your heart? If not, then take into account its transitory nature, for there is a 'treasure' which arises from a certain quality of life and is therefore more permanent.

In the *Genesis* parable *(chapter 1)*, humanity is given lordship over the animal kingdom, but only as God's representative. Much of humanity appears to have forgotten that responsible government must be undertaken in this spirit. While the great religions of the East have always declared that life should be lived in unity with all creation, Western culture has been slow to realise the limited resources of our world and how merciless exploitation can imperil life itself. At last we are beginning to think in terms of the 'global village' but our cult of consumerism needs to be changed. Work should enable us to live creatively so that we use and perfect our gifts and skills; and it should enable us to live with and for others so that we may join together in a corporate effort that benefits the whole.

Second: Gender This is a complex topic and cannot be dealt with adequately here. Women have fought for social and financial independence and also for some degre of sexual freedom, which has been made possible by modern methods of birth control. We have not yet achieved gender equality in the sense that men and women see and value each other for what they are and what they each contribute to the richness of living. In the Western world, we still live in a male orientated society whose roots are deep and subtle, despite superficial improvements. In some other parts of the world, women are relegated to a greatly inferior status and still have a long struggle ahead of them to achieve what liberty Western women enjoy.

For centuries the Christian church taught that sexual intercourse belonged only to marriage and that marriage could only be dissolved by the death of one of the partners. But there has been a great change of attitudes about this for now about 50% of people live together before they consider marrying and at least one in three marriages end in divorce.

We also live in a society that downgrades the value of sexual loving and wrongly uses sexual attraction for the advertisers' monetary gain. In the media the more brutal aspects of sexual behaviour have an increasing vogue, for violence is regarded as a 'selling' emotion. We are disturbed by revelations of child abuse and statistics which show how many women are battered or subject to violence in marriage. Yet despite all this, on the whole human beings are capable of tenderness, of sympathy and compassion, especially if they are inspired to be so.

Has Jesus anything to say about the gender question? He was not married and he had no children. His life as such was not the norm for he was consumed by a burning mission to bring in a new reign of God in people's lives being aware that he had very little time. We cannot treat his life as a literal example to be followed. Rather he was a catalyst for the heart of his life and teaching generates power for creative living. Considering his background, Jesus' vision was quite extraordinary. He was brought up on the mistaken Old Testament view that the male seed contained the perfectly formed human being while the woman's womb was the soil in which the seed was sown. Her role was passive. To waste the seed was wicked, hence homosexual relationships and masturbation were considered sinful, especially as children were essential to maintain the nation's survival. We have a different view because we know that the human embryo is formed by a union of both sexes and we need to control not expand the population. Yet Jesus saw sexual union as a sacrament; it was an act of loving bonding and

119

total commitment and as such it was permanent (*Mark 10*). But he also treated men and women on an equal basis when he argued that a man could commit adultery against his wife, a belief not found in Jewish law. He utterly condemned those who caused harm to children and less experienced adults (*Mark 9:42–49*). His opposition to divorce arises at least partly from his concern for the destitute, amongst them women and children whose husbands and fathers had left them penniless.

Two further points need to be borne in mind which explain the subordinate role of women in Christian thinking. By deifying Jesus the man, and propounding the doctrine of the Trinity, we have arrived at a masculine godhead – the father, the son and the sexless spirit. To provide some female principle, we elevate Mary, but as a virgin mother she is a model that cannot speak to women. Their experience of conception and childbearing comes through union with a man. It is also quite unproductive to claim that the Virgin Mary by her obedience to God's will, compensates for the disobedience of the first woman Eve. For many centuries women have had to bear the insulting identification with the temptress who led Adam astray, when physically there was no way in which they could identify themselves with Mary and emulate virgin motherhood.

But Jesus taught that God is spirit. Gender should only come into the godhead in so far as God is all embracing. Jesus the man, who through his life of love and fidelity became Christ, is one thing, but Jesus, God the Son is another matter entirely. Jesus the man, translated into the indwelling Christ-spirit, is free from gender implication because both genders are merely sub-divisions of humanity and the Christ spirit includes humanity itself. The whole point of the Father-son relationship which Jesus knew, is not its maleness but that it was a relationship of intimacy between the individual self and the great self. This relationship is what all the mystics of all faiths, genders and race have experienced. Unity with the divine spirit is possible, recognisable and to be sought after as the mainspring of joy and fulfilment. When Jesus answered the Sadducees' sardonic question about the woman who had seven husbands: whose wife would she be in heaven?, he said that life in the hereafter was free of sexual complications. It was 'as the angels'. The woman's role as child-bearer was no longer relevant.

Third: the misuse of power I have not been able to discuss the arms race or the appalling poverty in which nearly two thirds of the human race subsists. The two facts are not unconnected because the amount of money squandered in the build up of arms could solve most of the major world problems of hunger, malnutrition, disease and poverty. But we are living in times of hope now that the cold war seems to be a thing of the past and the superpowers are talking to each other about both nuclear and conventional

120

arms reductions. We have seen great advances through technological achievement and expertise but we are also becoming aware that some of these may have destructive consequences. Medical techniques have ensured that the human embryo can be fertilised outside the womb. Genetic engineering has already begun. We have to ask whether this is acceptable on moral and religious grounds. It is already being used in the production of our food, but the results may not be wholly justifiable. The excessive use of fertilisers and insecticides may produce unforeseen health hazards; organically produced food may have much to recommend it. The spiritual truth is that the earth is not our possession. We only inhabit it together with other living species. There are spiritual dimensions to life which we can only glimpse. We are finite, mortal creatures with both potential and limitation. Recognising these facts, we see that the human species has to become more mature if it is to cope with power. Jesus saw that humans have confused power with greatness. They have sought to exercise ultimate authority, wanting dominion, so that they could have others in subjection and could be looked up to and feted. He saw before him the absolute rulers of his time and the might of Rome, but his idea of greatness was in a different category. His concept of service has profoundly influenced individual human behaviour, but if it were more universally accepted what revolutionary progress might we make?

For many millions today, living is still simply a matter of survival, but in affluent Western society, with its abundant riches in the arts, music and literature, the majority can afford to seek for self-fulfilment and self-affirmation. These are good things in themselves but when they tip over into the desire for self-gratification even at the expense of others' needs, then danger threatens. Jesus' way has sometimes been presented as the way of self-mortification, discipline and denial. It may perhaps involve these things but only if they are demanded by the cause of truth and justice, for the sake of others. We are meant to live in partnership, in fellowship with each other, in giving and receiving and loving: this does entail the cost of rejecting self-centredness. We have much to learn about the structures of power, particularly its obsessiveness. Jesus seems to me to be the first modern human being – humanity as it is meant to be. I have also found that, by acknowledging him as such, some of the weaknesses in my own nature can be overcome. His way of love is hard but bright with joy and fulfilment and we do not walk it alone. If we wish, he walks with us all the time.

APPENDIX

A note on the Apocalyptic discourses

WE HAVE IN ALL THREE GOSPELS what is known as the **Apocalyptic discourse** by Jesus (*Mark 13 : 1–37 ; Luke 21 : 5–38 ; Matthew 24 : 5–38*). I do not propose to discuss this at all in detail as I believe it has little relevance for us today. Apocalypse is a Greek word standing for an unveiling of the future but it is less common than the Latin word, revelation. The supreme example of Jewish apocalyptic writing in the Old Testament is *Daniel*, and of Christian in the New Testament, *Revelation*.

People are always fascinated by trying to look into the future, especially if they are dissatisfied with the present. (Our own science fiction is a modern example of 'apocalypse' and some of it contains serious social comment.) Apocalyptic writing was a source of comfort and strength when life under tyranny and oppression became very hard to bear.
Jewish apocalyptic writing was very popular some centuries before and during the time of Roman occupation. But after the last uprising against Rome in AD 138, it died out. Christian apocalypses flourished during the first three centuries of persecution by the Roman authorities, then, when Christianity became the official religion of the empire, no more were written.

It is difficult to know how much Jesus himself was concerned with eschatology (doctrine of the Last Things, i.e. death, judgement, heaven and hell, end of the world). Scholarly opinion is not united on these matters, but Jesus' clear prophetic sense and intuitive apprehension told him when individual people were heading for disaster and he wept over the fate of his own nation who were refusing the way of peace and love which he offered. A study of '*Q*' shows that Jesus was deeply concerned about the future. He saw the present time as one of crisis, not only personally, and for his disciples, but also for his nation. His immediate disciples believed that their present age was coming to an end and that the end would come suddenly (cf. Paul in *1 Thessalonians 5 : 1* 'About dates and times, my friends, there is no need to write to you, for you yourselves know perfectly well that the day of the Lord comes like a thief in the night').

A detailed commentary on *Mark 13*, would suggest that it includes some genuine words of Jesus, which have become attached to an early Christian apocalypse, about the fate of Jerusalem and the future persecution of his disciples . The following extracts are some of those credited with being genuine Jesus:

'Learn a lesson from the fig tree. When its tender shoots appear and are breaking into leaf, you know that summer is near. In the same way when you see all this happening (disaster), you may know that the end is near, at the very door. . . . Yet about the day or hour (the end of the world) no one knows, not even the angels in heaven, not even the Son, no one but the Father. Be on your guard, keep watch. You do not know when the moment is coming'. Then follows the parable of the absent householder whose servants must always be ready for his homecoming. Finally, 'And what I say to you, I say to everyone: Keep awake' *(13:28–37)*.

Jesus may have believed that the end of the world was imminent. We do not know. His early disciples felt very strongly that this was so and had to adjust, as did Paul, when it did not happen in their lifetime. Nevertheless Jesus' words about alertness are fundamental to the human situation.

SI SONENT TUBÆ PARATUS